The Disappearance of the Outside

A MANIFESTO FOR ESCAPE BY

Andrei Codrescu

 Addison-Wesley
Publishing Company, Inc.

READING, MASSACHUSETTS
MENLO PARK, CALIFORNIA
NEW YORK   DON MILLS, ONTARIO
WOKINGHAM, ENGLAND   AMSTERDAM
BONN   SYDNEY   SINGAPORE   TOKYO
MADRID   SAN JUAN

Portions of Part Ten of this book first appeared in *City Lights Review*, 1987. Ideas developed in this book were explored in essays published in *Columbia: A Magazine of Poetry and Prose*, No. 14, 1989; *Tulane Architecture Review*, Summer 1989; *In This Corner: A Magazine of Fiction, Art, and Attitude*, Vol. 1, No. 5, June 1989; and *Organica*, Vol. 8, No. 27, Spring 1989.

Library of Congress Cataloging-in-Publication Data

Codrescu, Andrei, 1946–
    The disappearance of the outside : a manifesto for escape / by Andrei Codrescu.
        p. cm.
    ISBN 0-201-12194-8
    ISBN 0-201-57098-X (pbk.)
    1. Codrescu, Andrei, 1946–   —Biography.   2. Poets, American—20th century—Biography.   3. Romanian Americans— Biography.   4. Romania—Intellectual life.   I. Title.
PS3553.03Z4627   1990
811'.54—dc20   89-49310
[B]

Cover design by Gary Koepke
Text design by Copenhaver Cumpston
Set in 10 $\frac{1}{2}$ -point Palatino by Total Concept Associates, Brattleboro, VT

1 2 3 4 5 6 7 8 9-MW-9594939291
First printing, April 1990
First paperback printing, January 1991

Praise for *The Disappearance of the Outside*

"The book moves with swift energy, chances to laugh or linger over intriguing perspectives rising from page after glorious page."
San Diego Magazine

"Politics, philosophy, memoir, and literary criticism all commingle here with a peculiarly Eastern European sense of humor."
Booklist

"Codrescu deftly...uses his personal experience to lead into political, cultural, and philosophical commentary. [He] plays with ideas, extending and expanding them, and then passes them on to readers like batons."
Baltimore Sun

"Piercing critique of life and culture in the West and the prospectively deleterious consequences for a newly liberated Eastern Europe."
Washington Times

"For anecdote and absurdity, you will enjoy Codrescu's book. But beware. An intelligence and wit as keen as his is not content merely to be outside the cage of Romanian conformism. It has a restless, questing quality."
Newsday

"*The Disappearance of the Outside* makes a persuasive case that capitalist technocracy may accomplish what communist bureaucracy could not—the imprisonment of the human spirit."
Indianapolis Star

"Codrescu is engaging, amusing, and devastatingly accurate."
Newark Star-Ledger

"Codrescu is joyful; his writing enacts a love of freedom."
San Diego Tribune

"Unique and valuable in the perspective it gives us of one who has lived through the various forms oppression can take in this century."
Chicago Tribune

POETRY
License to Carry a Gun (1970)
The History of the Growth
    of Heaven (1971, 1973)
the, here, what, where (1972)
Secret Training (1973)
A Serious Morning (1973)
grammar & money (1973)
A Mote Suite for Jan & Anselm (1976)
The Lady Painter (1977)
The Marriage of Insult & Injury (1977)
For the Love of a Coat (1978)
Necrocorrida (1980)
Diapers on the Snow (1981)
Selected Poems 1970–1980 (1983)
Comrade Past & Mister Present (1986)

FICTION
Why I Can't Talk on the Telephone (1971)
The Repentance of Lorraine (1976)
Monsieur Teste in America & Other
    Instances of Realism (1987)

ESSAYS
A Craving for Swan (1986)
Raised by Puppets Only to Be
    Killed by Research (1989)

MEMOIRS
The Life & Times of an
    Involuntary Genius (1975)
In America's Shoes (1983)

TRANSLATIONS
For Max Jacob (1974)
At the Court of Yearning:
    Poems of Lucian Blaga (1989)

WORKS EDITED
American Poetry Since 1970: Up Late (1987)
The Stiffest of the Corpse:
    An Exquisite Corpse Reader (1989)

C O N T E N T S

I am writing this literally in the ruins of the Communist world, in my hometown of Sibiu, Romania. This beautiful Gothic city in the heart of Europe has been badly damaged by fighting. The old Cathedral, the Bruckenthal Museum, the shady squares of my youth, all bear the scars of the falling of the last red domino in Europe. (Not counting Albania, of course, which is in the clouds and the mountains and can only be reached by a ladder with rungs of bones.)

My scarred childhood still hides fleetingly in the damaged squares of my ghost town, calling forth its barely remembered shadows. It is here that I first heard the ancient German of my nurse Ilse, my grandmother's guttural smoky Hungarian, and the spring-clear Romanian of Lucian Blaga, Transylvania's greatest poet.

The greatest fight for liberty in Romanian history took

place in these parts in what seems like only moments ago. That is the great secret: only a few moments, only a *single* moment separate life from death, liberty from tyranny, the Outside from the inside. The people of the East—as I sometimes call this region and its mind in my book—have come Outside at long last after painful dark decades in the repressive interiors of police states. I have been waiting twenty years for this moment.

I wish that I could extend my happiness—and those of millions of others—into a far horizon of hope. As a member in good standing of LEV—Liberation Euphoria Vampires—I know, however, that the long road ahead is bumpy and that it leads, to my regret, into a new interior. This euphoric Outside will not, I believe, be long-lived. I base this assertion on the two halves of my life: the early half, spent here in Romania, and the next half, spent in the West. The thesis of this book, which is both personal and merely reflected, is that the two former oppositions of East and West will join together in a new electronic globe that is not a good thing for human beings. I attempt to show from two simultaneous sides how this future is coming about, and I propose a number of escapes from it through the use of Imagination.

Sibiu, Romania, December 31, 1989

Time
Before
Time

Its nature is that it's outside, outside the outside.
Not a vehicle but a motion. No meaning, no
   correlative,
no use, no rejection, no acceptance, no form, no
   intention,
no morality, no religion, no school, no forebears,
no value, no price, no time, no bones. It is its
own future and purpose, own audience and
   shill.
It has no nature. It has the world.

—George Evans, *Eyeblade*

One August evening in 1956, when I was ten years old, I heard a thousand-year-old shepherd wrapped in a cloak of smoke tell a story around a Carpathian campfire. He said that a long time ago, when time was an idea whose time hadn't come, when the pear trees made peaches, and when fleas jumped into the sky wearing iron shoes weighing ninety-nine pounds each, there lived in these parts a sheep called Mioritza.

The flock to which Mioritza belongs is owned by three brothers. One night, Mioritza overhears the older brothers plotting to kill the youngest in the morning, in order to steal his sheep. The young brother is a dreamer, whose "head is always in the stars." Mioritza nestles in his arms, and warns the boy about the evil doings soon to unfold, and begs him to run away. But, in tones as lyrical as they are tragic, the young poet-shepherd tells his beloved Mioritza to go see his mother after he is killed, and to tell her that he didn't really die, that he married the moon instead, and that all the stars were at his wedding. The boy then tells Mioritza the name of each star, where it came from, and what its job is, just in case the mother, who is not easily fooled, wants to know names and faces. Before morning, the older brothers murder the young shepherd, as planned. There is no attempt to resist, no counterplot, no new deviousness. Fate unfolds as foretold. The moon has a new husband, and the story must be known.

Mioritza wanders, looking for the boy's mother. But she tells everyone along the way the story as well. The murder was really a wedding, the boy married the moon, and all the stars were present. She names each star and explains where it came from. The Pleiades are bad girls who swept dust into the eyes of the sun. The Little Dipper feeds kind milk to the poor because it had once been an evil Titan who wasted his gold. Venus was once a vain queen who loved an evil angel. The circle of Orion is made of girls who can't stop dancing. There are carpenters, witches, and smiths up there, worlds of people transformed and made forever exemplary. Mioritza knows everyone in the sky. She never tires of the story. She laments the death of her beloved with stories of the origin of the worlds.

Her wandering takes her across the rivers of the Carpathian mountains to the Black Sea, a path that describes the natural border of Romania. Her migration defines the space of the people, a space the Romanian poet Lucian Blaga called "mioritic." Mioritza herself is the moving border of the nation, a storytelling border whose story is borderless and cosmic. She calls into being a place and a people that she circumscribes with narrative. She causes geography to spring from myth, she contains within her space-bound body the infinity of the cosmos.

The old shepherd leaned on his crooked stick by the flames, speaking slowly and monotonously, without stress or drama, words that had been in place since before the beginning of time. I had the eerie thought that this shepherd must have been one of the killers, one of the older brothers, whose punishment was to live for eternity, following Mioritza, repeating her tale. Now and then a giant firefly soared from the other side of the mountain, and there was rumbling like thunder. Whenever this happened, the old man stopped talking to roll his tobacco and to check the bright stars that in those days were bigger and more numerous than they are today. Around midnight it got very warm, and the old man said that there were so many ghosts interested in this tale that they were crowding, ghostly shoulder to ghostly shoulder, folding inside one another accordionlike, making the mournful thunder that could be heard in the valley. There, the city people huddled close, not knowing what scared them, and their heat rose into the mountain to warm us.

The telling lasted all night and at times the story was a raft drifting between stars and sheep with my boy's body aboard. The real sheep slept around me, jammed against one another, a soft, dark mass of unconsciousness from whose dreams the old man wove the tale. By dawn everyone was asleep—except me and my friend Ion. We stayed awake until the stars faded in the sky and did not go to sleep until Mioritza said: "Now you heard my tale, go and always tell it!" Ion and I thus became responsible for the transmission of this late variant of the legend of Mioritza of the Transylvanian Alps in the year 1956 when, from the western side of the mountain, we saw the flares and heard the rumble of tanks and felt the heat of burning villages from neighboring Hungary.

Mioritza's timeless tale spun in its capsule of sparks and smoke above the sparks and smoke men made in history. We who were in the mountains and in the story were above the world as long as the story lasted. When the story stopped, the world roared in.

Mioritza begins her tale, like other myths of origin, with an incantation intended to suspend time and to remove her listeners from the common world. "When the pear tree made peaches" was long ago, but it is easy to get there if you follow the story. Mioritza begins by talking to herself as if no one else were listening: "Fair Mioritza, soft Mioritza, tell your tale. . . ." She is truly "spinning a yarn," a weaving that eventually takes in her listeners. When we are "spun," we exit the world of history, corruption, and time. We have been transported, in Mircea Eliade's words, into *illo tempore*, into that time before time when gods made worlds from words. Once upon a time, when there was no time, when time was an idea whose time had not yet come, all gestures were fertile, all words were magical, every act had eternal consequences, the cosmos could not help but be endlessly generative.

Yes, once upon a time there was plenty of time for everything. The immensity of childhood made the borders of time as improbable as the world of school that Ion and I knew we had to return to in the fall. Inside the shepherd's story there prevailed an order different from the one in the "real" world. The journey we undertook with Mioritza was magical and complicated. We were always lost and always home. The images she showed us found homes in us as if there had been holes already there for them to fit in. The stars were already in us. She called them into being by naming them. In the enchanted light of the telling, we were a sieve of possibility: each star streamed through us seamlessly. We were the passageway for stories coming from her world into ours, though it wasn't possible to say which world was which—which was outside, which inside. If there were an "outside" anywhere, it was the remote one we were expected to return to, the one we were doomed to spend our lives in along with everyone else, the so-called reality of city and school and parents. Nothing seemed more unreal to us than that "reality" while we lived in the inside-outside cosmos of the story. In the light of this measureless feeling, reality was a temporary and incomprehensible agreement.

Why did we have to go back? It was—and still is—the question. We had found the place where the original ontological *why* had been resolved. In the story, by the fire, we knew why we existed, why we were "us" and not "they" ("us" being those who knew the story, and "they" the uninitiated outside the circle), why the world was the way it was. And having found the answers, we did not understand why we had to go back to a world where those answers still had not been given or were not understood or were, most likely of all, forbidden.

The old story was a time machine that abolished time. But it was a machine nonetheless. Just as it is now possible to imagine a whole new order of "mechanical" human beings, cyborgs that erase the borders between man and what he creates, it was possible then to glimpse in stories a whole other order of "machines," mythic ones that erased the borders between man and what created him.

I on stayed in Romania where he is a professor of literature at the University of Cluj, a job that, undoubtedly, offers him many opportunities to footnote the myth of the lovelorn sheep. I left the country and changed languages but have not stopped telling Mioritza's tale. Ion and I have merely divided the job: he maintained it inside the borders of a modern police state called "Romania," while I kept it outside of them. Our parallel renderings form another border, peculiar to our time, two strands of electrified barbed wire between which lies the no-man's-land of politics. Unlike the border drawn by Mioritza's wandering, which is eternal, the border that divides Ion and me is historical. Our stories issue divided from Mioritza's story like the ever-diverging twin spirals of a ram's horns. One of us is inside, the other outside. But which is which?

B ack in the city, the other order reigned. "You don't know your place!" shouted my mother. Those were words hovering above my head like a large pterodactyl from my first-grade reader, ready to snatch me off somewhere where I *would* know my place. Whether I spoke daringly, out of turn, or impertinently (I mostly did), or whether I voiced my suspicions plainly and calmly, the response was always that it wasn't my place to speak, that I was speaking out of place, and that, simply, I didn't *know* my place.

What was my place? Was my place not the place where I was? Was the place that my voice inadvertently trespassed upon not *my* place as well? Was I not always and naturally in place? What was this place that I belonged to that was different from the adults' place? Were there distinctly drawn borders between my place and theirs? And how was I to know what my place was? Negatively? By learning what *wasn't* my place? Perhaps what was really meant was that *my* place didn't in fact exist or that, if it did, it was confined to certain conventional ideas indulgently ceded by tradition to children.

I had been allowed to sleep in my mother's bed until I was nine but then it suddenly wasn't my place to be in there. This was a decision I made myself because I had been dreaming every night that my mother, who was young and pretty, was turning into a frozen witch after I fell asleep. Her body of ice encased me in a frightening blue sheet of cold. I woke up in the morning unable to move, until ministered to with hot chamomile tea gently rubbed on the eyelids by my, once again, young and pretty mother. Nearly smothered to death by the return of an interior which may or may not have been Edenic, I made a narrow escape from my mother's bed into a cubicle I shared with my cousins.

My cousins, a boy and a girl, both younger than I, were not allowed in the daytime into what we called "our room." Only at night, in our beds, when we went to sleep, was it really "our room." But while we were sleeping we were not strictly speaking in "our room": we were elsewhere, in dreams. Dreams, like the story, were spacious. In them we were once more simultaneously outside and inside.

We were not allowed to run in the hallways past the closed doors of certain other forbidden rooms. We were enjoined even from streaming past the *entrances* to these places where we didn't belong at any time. One would have to have been born in the last gasp of the dying Austrian empire (still dying after World War II!) to appreciate the dark propriety of a bourgeois house (even under the Communists!), with its shabby but still massive Biedermeier armoires towering over young Sigmund Freud (alive in every child of such a household!).

In our house—which, by virtue of certain numbers in front and some recognizable architectural oddities was the first place I had learned belonged to me, or rather that I was of it—the kitchen belonged to my grandmother. I was shooed out of there as quickly as I stuck my pointy (questioning) little head in the door. My grandmother wielded a perpetually bloody knife which had always just been withdrawn from the gentle innards of a lamb, a rabbit, or a chicken. There were onions frying about her with a sound like that of rain on a fire. At the end of the kitchen was the small door to the pantry, where preserved on shelves for darker times were rows and rows of dried fruit, preserves, pickled cabbage, sacks of flour, tins of oil, sugar, and vinegar. This was the place I would have dearly loved to let myself into, but first I would have had to lull my grandmother to sleep with opium tea, remove the knife from her hands, and not tarry very long. This I was unable to do, although once I had gone so far as to hide under her voluminous skirt and to crawl out under the table all the way to the first ropes of garlic by the pantry door. But then she caught me, and the kitchen became officially out of bounds.

The privy was a frightening and dark affair that we shared with another family, fat monsters who spent mysterious hours in there with foreign language magazines while we hopped about on one foot in front. When I could slide in at last it was into a hollow of stink, cigar smoke, and alien mind processes, all of which I endeavored to erase in order to do my business freely. I told myself stories within that demonic dark, stories that were vehicles, little cars that whizzed out of there with me inside, fueled by spinning and imagining.

I was forbidden to use the living room because only visitors were ushered in there. Its strictly-for-show piano was a stubborn symbol of better days when my grandmother, as a little girl, had performed for solemn Victorians. The glass cabinets filled with religiously dusted porcelain plates were always submerged in a mysterious half-cool twilight. Some kind of blue Saxon ducks slid over their mirrored surfaces. I used to sneak into that room, perfectly conscious of my transgression, hide under the piano, and experience intense bliss, the beginnings, I'm sure, of sexuality. It was under that piano, in fact, at the age of ten (the fall after the summer I spent in the mountains), that I beheld the splendor of my schoolmate Dora's unshadowed slit, while she beheld my equally blameless rod. To be doing such a thing was most definitely not our place, in every conceivable sense of the word: as geography, as act, as age. The current that passed between us was as timeless as the magic of the tale, but it was more closely bordered by the world, more furtive and more difficult. On the mountain the cosmos had streamed leisurely in, abolishing the world completely. Under the piano it had to roar over the narrow bed of liberty we had carved out of the prison we lived in.

That left the outdoors. As soon as we woke up from our separate dreams, my cousins and I were sent "outside." We loved the outside, which consisted of the yard with the tree and the capped well in it and the street in front of the house where strangers promenaded, flirting. We loved it but we also despised it because it was somehow "inferior" to the inside of the house whence we had been banished. Banishment had divided the world into the outside, which was "our place," and the inside of the house which was too good for us, therefore not "our place." "Good" was not for us.

At times, a curious reversal took place. When we did something bad, we were told to go "inside." We were forbidden to play outside. This was a dire punishment indeed because no matter how "superior" the inside was to the "outside," it was horrifying to go inside on a beautiful day, particularly since, once there, we could not touch or play with anything because it wasn't "our place." The loss of the outdoors was terrible. We would have preferred to stay outside in any weather if the alternative was being made to be quiet inside. Outside one could shout and be "bad." No one made us be quiet out there. Our voices, no matter how loud, were home outside. Inside, one had to hush up "because of the neighbors," or because one was too loud or inappropriate or forward. The inside, it seemed, was the place where everything was circumscribed, diminished, made smaller. As long as we were children and thus incapable of appreciating the fine limitations of the interior, it wasn't our place, though we lived there. The outdoors, by contrast, demanded that we run, shout, twirl, cover distance, and generally augment our capacities as much as possible. Even if the inside had once been carved from the outside, as a city is carved from a forest, or a house from a field, they had now parted company for so long that they had very little left in common. The inside had redefined itself by its differences to the outside it had once been part of. But the outside didn't give a damn. Or so it seemed to us, for whom the street was the most immediate outside. For most citizens, the street was definitely inside the city, however, and there was a policeman patrolling it. The sort of outside that most of us would have agreed was definitely outside was the Carpathian peak where Mioritza's tale was being told. But alas, even there, the economics of sheep production and the price of cheese surrounded shepherd and mountain with the prison bars of their imperatives. In so-called reality the only operating terms were limiting. Only in the story was there a true Outside, though it too might have appeared confined behind the bars of grammar to someone determined to deny its existence. Even at that age, however, I was determined to find the Outside, not deny it, and that remains the job.

I early surmised that there were two kinds of "bad": an existential "bad" that was connected entirely to us children, and for which we had been banished from the house to the inferior outside of the street, and a situational "bad" for which we were plucked from the wild outdoors and banished to the civilized inside. Our existential "bad" doomed us to that inferior place that was ours (and which we loved) while situational "bad" was an exemplary lesson in feeling our unworthiness amid the superior place that was not ours (but which we also loved and felt guilty for defiling). Being situationally bad doomed us to living allegorically, allegory being the symbolic place that guilt carves out of love. Our existential badness, however, was literal and total: the inmates of hell just don't know any better; they frolic as if there were no tomorrow. The cursed outside was our home, while our home in the approved inside was a place of exile. Our children's existence took place under the double sign of this paradox that divided the world into ours and not ours, with bad and good attached but reversed in allegory and reality. The utopia (no place) of home (inside) met the existence (being) of the outside, though both were a story, an allegory that made no sense other than assigning moral values to both, and confusing us forever.

It so happened, for reasons more psychological than allegorical, that the story of my journey from womb to adolescence was one of increasing delight in the outside and growing horror of interiors. Home, school, society were interiors. The outside was outside: the mountains, Mioritza, wandering, stories, the streets, wherever the wrong bus went.

The books of my childhood, which followed the tales of that summer and the piano of that fall, were also time machines. I started reading early but I don't remember any books prior to the winter of my tenth year. When the heavy snowfall of 1956 came, covering the blood on the streets of Hungary, I was snug and warm on the other side of the mountain, buried in Jules Verne's *Twenty Thousand Leagues Under the Sea*. My mother and stepfather came and went, tracking mud and snow into the foyer. Once I saw a burly man give my mother an immense revolver. They whispered out of earshot, and I hoped that Othello, my stepfather, wouldn't hear about it. I was hoping also that somewhere in the silent depths of the ocean there would be something as vast and as complete as the time machine of the Carpathian shepherd.

Jules Verne evidently hoped for the same thing. I

escaped in books from the world of my parents and from school, but I was puzzled by books. I thought that stories ought to be "one night long." I wanted a tale to last from here to there at least like "a day's walk," if not a whole night's journey. It was not the night magic, the starry sky, and the ancient voice that I wanted, though certainly I missed them, but something else inside the stories themselves. Time had been made cosmic by the old shepherd, and I stubbornly insisted in measuring things by it. A book might take anywhere from a week to ten days to read but I could not live *completely* within it. To be sure, I would be someplace in a book whenever I was wanted. I would respond monosyllabically if possible and feign deafness if not (in Captain Nemo's sub, after all, the walls were made of cork).

But something was not well with books. They were sick in a way; they had been made in time and they were of it. Grown-ups could make you close the book to rejoin the "real" world. Books rarely gave you the feeling that *you might never come back*, for instance, which was always a possibility in the mountains. Books had a definite beginning and end and a spine and a shape and they cost money, or you had to take them back to the library. Their only advantage was that you could return to them and find the familiar places still there. That was a miracle for the sake of which one might overlook their other, patently temporal, qualities, and the partial loss of eternity thereby.

One day I had a revelation. There had been hints for some time that certain books had better not be discussed. Our next-door neighbor had a German Bible hidden at the bottom of an old sea chest. Her son Peter, who was a year older than me, showed it to me in secret one afternoon after making me swear that I would never reveal its existence to anyone. It was a heavy thing with tarnished copper clasps, gritty parchment pages, and sharp, black Gothic-script letters. It emitted a dark, pungent odor of darkness, monks, time, Gutenberg, sea journeys, incense, and last rites. Peter told me that there were other books like this, some old, some new, all of them containing secrets so awesome we would be put in prison for merely mentioning them. The clues soon multiplied: another schoolmate showed me a yellowed pamphlet entitled *Women's Bodies in Art*. It had been printed before the war, and the women, who were all nude, had been gathered from the ceilings of far-off cathedrals, French palaces, and Flemish galleries, and made to parade, three per page, before our astonished adolescent eyes. Even more shocking was a little book printed during the war that had a swastika on the cover, dangling from the chest of a uniformed soldier. This book was kept in the darkest stacks of our public library behind a door that was usually locked but was unlocked one day when Peter and I tried it. The swastika book was the only one we had time to see before we heard footsteps and had to retreat swiftly into the public room which was full of light and approved books. I realized that there existed all about me a world of forbidden books.

I assumed that whatever was missing in the books I was allowed to read could no doubt be found in the ones I wasn't. There was the key to my loss. When I found out that the books I was not allowed to read were also forbidden to grown-ups, I became certain that a secret library existed but was, like certain passes in the mountains, hard to find, inaccessible. Its books were, like the shepherds, rare beings to whom access was restricted.

Even the books that we were allowed to see and read were treated in some measure as sacred objects. In bookstores they stood behind stout glass cases, a setting that belied their flimsy pages and bad printing. Not returning a book to the library on time carried such dire punishments that one wouldn't dream of such a thing. One boy who kept a library book was taken out of school one day by his parents, and the only answer we could obtain as to his fate was a wistful shake of the head on the part of our teachers. I did hear later that his parents had also been removed to a remote province for unspecified "crimes against the State," one of which, no doubt, was their son's crime. And, finally and simply, there were not that many books: a "paper shortage," falsely invoked by the regime, made icons of all available books. Unlike the shepherds' stories, which lodged themselves between my ears and there made themselves a permanent home (or one that would last as long as I did), books suffered from the fragility of matter. There was a difference in what they told as well. Books were terribly careful to stay in the world. Even fairy tales felt obliged in print to establish some kind of credibility in the "reality" the oral tales dismissed. Their "onceuponatimes" were predictable, not sudden and chilling as they'd been in the mountains. Books made a bargain with the "reality" I had no taste for. Their business seemed to be in the world even when they were fantastic. If the shepherd's tale was a sacred machine working in magic time, books were profane machines, which is to say machine machines, like the machines that made cans and wheels. As objects they could be bought and exchanged and each copy was exactly like the next. They were part of the (admittedly difficult) commerce we conducted amid shortages, but they were no different from cheese, fruit, or chickens.

Cheese, fruit, and chickens are serious things. For books to exist on the same level was a guarantee of their gravity. As a child I never questioned their currency. An unspoken regional belief held that currency high. In Transylvania we have an ontological blood relation to the book. Our famed prince, Vlad the Impaler, later known as Dracula (son of the devil), ruler of Wallachia in the mid-fifteenth century, was the founder of our nation and the inventor of a number of refined technologies of murder, including impaling on a stake. During his terrible reign, he attacked and sacked several times my hometown of Sibiu—once known by its German name of Hermannstadt—in central Transylvania.

Hermannstadt was a German merchant town, well known for its strong guilds of craftsmen. The good burghers of Hermannstadt did not enjoy being impaled, any more than they liked paying taxes. When Dracula ordered a number of them to have dinner with him amid the forest of stakes that held their wailing and dying neighbors, quite a few of them became sick. For this infraction, Dracula ordered them impaled on stakes higher than the rest so they wouldn't have to smell the carnage. Dracula's sense of humor, harsh even by medieval standards, became legendary when the burghers commissioned a number of German printers, contemporaries of Gutenberg (who had just invented a means of reproducing a book mechanically), to issue pamphlets on Dracula's atrocities.

Gutenberg's invention put thousands of monks out of work and, in the end, also put the Middle Ages out of business. The first book Gutenberg made several of was the Bible. But the next wave of printed books were made on assignment for the burghers of Hermannstadt. The earliest account is a 1485 reprint of news sheets published originally in the year of Dracula's attack on Hermannstadt, 1462, entitled *About a Wild Tyrant Called Dracole Wayda Who MCCCCLVI Years After the Birth of Our Lord Jesus Christ Carried Out Many Terrible and Wondrous Deeds in Wallachia and Hungary*, published by Bartholomeus Gothan in Lübeck. This pamphlet contained tale after tale of the gruesome and cruel doings of the Walachian prince, and was Bram Stoker's chief inspiration.

These pamphlets were instant best-sellers. They were in fact the world's first best-sellers, the world's first mass-market books, the beginning of literacy and thus ancestors of capitalism, parliamentarianism, communism, and bourgeois democracy.

Dracula himself, who unified his kingdom by wresting power from feudal lords, was an influence on Ivan the Terrible, who first read his story in a Russian version written by monks in the fifteenth century, and published under the name *Povesty o Mutyanskom Voyevode Drakule*. Dracula's fierce nationalism and ruthlessness also inspired Machiavelli's *The Prince*. Dracula exemplified the advantages of central power over fragmentation, and thus laid the foundation for a philosophy of the national state. The Gutenberg-era pamphlets were remarkable foreshadowings of technology's lack of ideological bias. Dracula, the myth invented by aggrieved merchants, became the basis for the vampire of Bram Stoker, while Dracula the politician invented nationalism, which is also a form of vampirism, whereby the terrible suction of central government drains the life from the loose, autonomous city-states. The modern world was born from the dual text of a provincial Balkan ruler: the fascination of reading began the drive toward centralization and mechanization.

Prince Dracula was eventually arrested by an expeditionary force sent by the Hungarian king as a result of the bad publicity, and the burghers were satisfied. The first mass media had also scored its first judicial coup, and the law began an unholy alliance with mechanical reproduction—that is, with propaganda.

Dracula notwithstanding, Romania was not a country until the mid-nineteenth century. After the revolution of 1848, which ended hundreds of years of Turkish and Turco-Greek domination, it hastened to join Europe. Its literature rose fiercely from historical chronicle and pamphlet into poetry. Between 1910 and 1948 Romanians absorbed books the way eggplant absorbs olive oil, and produced them as well, a literary gush comparable to that of their contemporaries, the oil wells of Ploesti.

When the Communists came to power after the war, the flow of books was stemmed, both from within and from without. State policy at the time of my birth in 1946 was a Dracula-like activity of cultural impalement. First, the authors were victimized (prison, murder, silence), then their books (burning, banning, oblivion).

At the age of fourteen, four immense towers of time removed from Mioritza, I had become a reading monster, a master of the flashlight and of sleepwalking. I was also obsessed with all the books I wasn't supposed to read. I knew that they couldn't have all disappeared, because people winked when I brought them up. They were about me, hidden like swamp treasures, their nocturnal flickering full of mystery and promise.

In one of the cafés where we potential literati met for Turkish coffee and lemon ice, I met a dapper older man who lived near our lycée. Dr. M, as we called him, was a former novelist and professor, forcibly retired some years before for, once again, unspecified "crimes against the State." He was wrapped in a funereal cloak, a hooded coat from another century, with deerhorn buttons and large, bulging pockets. He needed only a monocle to shine above his well-combed white goatee to transform him into a personage from the heyday of *la belle époque*. He lived on a measly state pension in a little house all but lost in a walled garden grown wild. Dr. M invited Ion and me to his house. The entrance was unprepossessing and humble, covered with a trellis of dying roses. But the inside! On the walls were Byzantine icons, folk weavings, abstract paintings, nude drawings. On little tables were folk carvings and neoclassical nudes.

Bookshelves everywhere groaned with books. All the hitherto invisible writers were on these shelves, and in complete editions: here were the poetry and philosophy of Lucian Blaga, the poems and writings of Ion Barbu, Matei Caragiale, Ion Vinea. It was as if we'd been suddenly transported to another world, compared to which the shabby one we lived in was but two-dimensional bleakness. All the books dated from the mythical era that ended just before our own began. Ion and I stepped from one world into another like characters in a fairy tale. Dr. M lived here in brilliant solitude, surrounded by the steam of his copper coffeepot and the glow of books. When the rains started that autumn, I found myself thinking, as I listened to their steady drone on the small windows, that Ion and I had been chosen among thousands of other questers for a magical journey that started here.

We began to read. I came to understand, after reading several poets, particularly Ion Barbu's hermetic work, that certain writers made extremely fine distinctions. They drew haughty lines between mere words and poetry, for instance. Literature conceived as a world of its own was news to me. The Party held that all words must serve the people. But here were words that served only language, a heightened and specific language at that. The secret of modern literature, and the reason why it was forbidden, was its autonomy.

Here once more was a sacred realm like Mioritza's, which made no bargains with the profane. These poets, made even more potent by interdiction, turned back the world-bound tales I had lived with since my summer in the mountains. They reversed the direction of time, pointing it once more toward eternity. This was the forbidden direction (as the authors themselves were), and in finding it I thought that I had regained my magical machine.

To give you an idea of the official drivel competing with

my poets, here is a "social realist" story produced in the Stalinist 1950s, published on the front page of a leading literary newspaper. It was entitled "Proletarian Love."

During the terrible days of Capitalism, the young baby boy of a dirt-poor family was abandoned in a trough outside the one-room shack. A pig came and ate the baby's genitals. The baby grew up to be a passionate Communist and a great worker in a steel factory. He was such a great worker that the Party Secretary, herself a passionate Communist, fell in love with him. When the inevitable confession came, she was taken aback. But after a thorough examination of her political conscience she decided to allow nothing to stand in their way. They were married, and together, in their great happiness, they fulfilled the five-year-plan in a mere two.

There is something deeper here than the obvious moral that the happiness of working for the State is greater than that of sex, namely, that a being emasculated by poverty can be regenerated by the work ethic. These lovers are so resolutely pointed toward earth, all possibilities of happiness are removed from the very beginning. This is the opposite of a fairy tale: the "happily ever after" has become voluntary servitude. Granted, not everything in our literature was this absurd, or this metaphorically clean. In the 1950s, the main task was to enclose the mind completely in Statespeak's barbed wire. The ubiquitous red leatherbound books of Comrade Stalin were everywhere. Stalin had written a book on every subject of importance: mathematics, biology, linguistics, art, literature. I thought (and was not alone) that somehow *every* book had been written by Stalin. And if not by him personally (though that *was* the point), at least under his tutelage. His substance, Stalinium, was the *effluvium vitae,* the substance that animated everything. His collected works stretched across every wall of the Russian bookstore Kniga Russkaya in my town.

This Russian bookstore at the center of Sibiu was a

curious place: no one frequented it. It was cold, empty, and frightening. The cold was from air conditioning, an unfamiliar sensation and technology in our town. No self-respecting Romanian would have been caught dead in this place, but I was curious and I liked to go there in the summer, both because it was cool and because I was intrigued by the mystery of a place of books that nobody read in a strange language that everyone despised. Nonetheless, both this language and these books were officially the "source of light," as both Russian and Stalin were referred to in my classes. This paradox of the existence of a vacated interior masquerading as the official fullness was a perfect adolescent problem. It was a model for other emptinesses disguised as fullnesses, other "lights" that served only to obscure. Kniga Russkaya was the Sphinx of my provincial Egypt. Loud Red Army marches blared from the store turntable. The clerks regarded me coldly, sensing in me a spy and a thief (I stole cold air) and a Jew. Most adults had a nose for this sort of thing: Jew, reader.

When I at last boycotted Kniga Russkaya (I was overcome by shame), I tried to recapture the mystery by going to churches. Like books, churches had about them an air both forbidding and irresistible. The few old people who frequented them on Sundays wrapped themselves in black from head to foot and moved silently in and out of their great doors with faces cloaked in sadness. My parents had never whispered a word to me about religion, but I picked up hints from my wondrous books. An idea of divinity that was far from taking shape as "God" was beginning to preoccupy me, and I felt that the solution might possibly be in these swollen, grotesque, empty buildings that stood vacant in various melancholy corners of my ancient burg. The great Teutsch Cathedral, built in the fourteenth century, was central to my reveries. I loved its great Gothic arches, the resolute spire pointing into the blue summer sky, and its scores of carved angels and demons perched heavily on cornices and eaves. I was attracted here too by the cold, and by silence and darkness. The tension between my self and the various houses of mystery I was discovering was immensely magnified by the cold. I later considered the peculiar frigid darkness of Kniga Russkaya and the Teutsch Cathedral more important than either Knowledge or God, their overt products. Great reserves of cold are needed to maintain distinct official realities.

In contrast with the mausoleum of dead propaganda books and the smoky angels of churches, my older friend's house, where all the forbidden books were, was warm, alive, and full of light. He let me borrow his books one by one, fully aware that he would go to prison if discovered. My friend Ion and I often speculated on the old man's motives. We advanced the proposition that he was homosexual. He would stand awfully close when enraptured by verses (he knew thousands of lines by heart), and his breath would come in rapid bursts that seemed somewhat out of proportion to even the most sublime poetry. No matter. The poetry *was* sublime, and if our sublime youthful presence was greater than that of books, that too makes sense. Dr. M was genuinely eager to expose us to books, an activity that was metasexual, as well as sexual. The discovery of forbidden books was for us intimately coupled with danger and with the question of sex. The chill of the many-headed mystery that had seized me was sexual in the extreme. I read secretly, like I masturbated.

I also became aware that hidden everywhere among us were people feeding on forbidden books. To pick the secret readers out of the crowd became the great game. I studied strangers like maps to try to discover the surreptitious reader in them. Certain of their features seemed to mark them clearly: a certain turn of the mouth, a gaze that pointed inward. I shadowed my secret intellectuals in the street, listened in on them in coffeehouses. I was drunk with the feeling of being part of a secret society. The Cambodian Communists learned to read for "intellectuals" in much the same way in the 1970s. Everyone wearing eyeglasses was murdered. They thought that faces marked by reading, like hands marked by farm work, could be read at a glance. Woe unto the secret reader!

The few books of literary rather than purely propagan- distic value that the Party let be published—conservative but honest artistic achievements by writers unwilling to rock the red boat—were published only grudgingly, and in editions too small to meet popular demand. The books that were not allowed were so much more numerous, so much more substantial to me, that no comparison could be made between official and forbidden books. Also, the world of forbidden books was not limited to existing books. I had seen only a fraction of these, but I believed in so many more that I experienced (as if I'd read them) books that didn't exist, that couldn't exist, books that came from the future or the past or another dimension. I could conjure invisible books from the air and absorb them through my skin into myself. I experienced thousands of books by this process of psycho-osmosis, books that came into being via my imagi- nation, and that would one day demand to be written.

I was not the only one to experience and imagine them. Thousands of people did (and do). All those imaginary books will come into being one by one. Where else but in a country where books are viewed this way will people line up at five in the morning outside a bookstore when there is a rumor that a new book of poems by a daring young poet will go on sale that day? People also line up at that early hour for cheese, fruit, and chicken, but spiritual hunger is felt every bit as keenly.

Kniga Russkaya was a microcosm of what surrounded us, namely, Russia. That is where the big silence and the cold came from. Solzhenitsyn tells how for many years he buried the manuscripts of his books in bottles in the woods, or hid them inside walls. I also heard of a man in a Romanian prison who wrote an entire novel on the single sheet of paper he had. To the uninitiated eye, that sheet looked just like a solid block of darkness. And yet, hidden in that spidery writing was a multilayered, intricately folded world.

The official house of words with its guard towers looked over a silent world inhabited by forbidden books and secret writers and readers. The Janus-faced censors in the towers had to look both outside and inside their domain for unauthorized books. In addition they had to define and maintain the official ideology they were sworn to defend. It was not an easy job, particularly since no one, at least in Romania, was doing it with any particular zeal. After Stalin had written all the books, only exegetes and enforcers were left. Our schoolteachers, forced to parrot the line of the textbooks, were bored out of their minds, as were we. The immense boredom into which I was born was an ideal conductor for the forbidden and the transcendent. The (real) penalties meted for breaching this boredom made it all worthwhile: my world was made to order for adolescent rebellion. I viewed my teachers and the countless Party small-fry who ran everything as insects (particularly since I'd read Kafka). These bugs were trying to confine my world with their unconvincing edicts because they were not well. They were ill.

The censor was a flawed person because he could not be entirely loyal. To be so, he'd have to have had an exact idea of what he was being asked to forbid, and the State could not provide one. Consequently, he embarked upon his enterprise of interdiction with only the vaguest of guidelines, and found that he had to *invent* the enemy. The use of imagination, even under such minimal conditions, was self-defeating because imagination, once kindled, could not be extinguished. The censor, at the mercy of his blazing imagination, began to see enemies everywhere while beset simultaneously by the suspicion that they did not exist at all. This sort of paranoia followed by radical doubt eventually became self-paranoia and self-doubt: the censor questioned his own existence. He became invisible to himself at certain times and in various degrees, states for which he compensated by making himself extremely visible and dangerous at other times. These moods determined the weather and *depth* of censorship.

There was a horizontal and a vertical dimension of censorship, forming a peculiar cross. At the center of the cross was the *Index Maleficorum*, the index of forbidden books. When the index was backed actively by the police, our intellectuals experienced a dizzying vertical: the basements of torture palaces. Later, in the 1960s, when Stalinist rigidity dissolved, the index became expansive and without muscle, horizontal. The horizontal was self-imposed more often than not. Self-censorship was policed by the shadows of policemen in the imagination. The vertical had been generative of transcendental hope: the harder the repression, the more exalted the upturned vision. The horizontal infested the ideology with insecurity, lessening the terror but increasing the boredom.

Throughout my adolescence we watched censorship like the weather: cloudy today, rainy tomorrow. Our writers were afflicted in various ways. The truly censored were invisible because they had been written out of every record. The names of Romanian writers in exile, for instance, were never mentioned. A law had been secretly passed that certain writers' names could never be used in print, *not even in crossword puzzles*. Until December 21, 1989, I was one of these writers. It amuses me very much to think that some-where in the gloom and misery of daily life in yesterday's Romania, some desperate soul might have attemped to attack the regime by inscribing my name in a crossword puzzle. "Lives in New Orleans & still thinks of his youth, and Dr. M. Eight letters."

That's easy! More tragically, there were imprisoned writers whose traces had been completely erased. And others yet, who lived suspended between prison and condi-tional liberty while working menial jobs, and who were forbidden to write anything of their own. Frequent raids assured their compliance. These persecuted souls became, by that perverse process that oppression always sets in motion, our true heroes. Their banning had elevated and ennobled them, and we sat dutifully at their rejected feet, listening to autumn rains drown the world, waiting for the future. That future, I am glad to say, has come to the sad iron chamber of Romania, at long last.

The self-censored, who pursued a life without intellec-tual minefields, suffered from tameness. They were timid academics who kept their jobs through endless kowtowing and mandarin reasoning. Their conservative forms were quite well crafted, hiding the empty insides. Content had vacated them, leaving in its wake a sterile virtuosity that was the subject of endless, equally sterile reviews.

The self-censored kept the literary machine grinding on to no one's surprise, pleasure, or delight. They turned up dutifully at congresses, readings, conferences, and rallies, their puffed-up, gray faces with large dark circles under heavy horn-rimmed glasses. Their air of weariness was a signal to the world to leave them alone so that they could start drinking. The self-censored drank themselves to death at the red-clothed tables of the Writers' Union, in dives, and at home. When they traveled abroad, their first order of business was getting expensive booze to drink. It was their payoff for years of restraint, deliberate suppression of talent, thought, and life. When they remembered their souls—smothered in fat and vodka—they tried to help. Occasionally, they would provide the fog in which those pursued by the censor and the police could hide in. They would sometimes interpose their soft alcoholic bodies between a real writer and his pursuers. Rarely successful, they drew great praise for their selfless acts which were, most often, only mild suicide attempts. The self-censored lied, but they were so unconvincing that every word they wrote was the opposite of what they would have liked everyone to believe. They served as weather vanes. Their only hope, and one that was, alas, being realized, was that eventually everyone would exhibit the same ambiguous, ironic disposition. At that point the lie moved on to a new level, where it was authenticated by ubiquity. Foreign journals and books were confiscated at the border, not because of their content but because they conferred status to the censor who could display them on his coffee table. Too amorphous to hurt, too ambiguous to catch, too faceless to love, the self-censored flowed heavily, as a sort of intellectual molasses, into the life of the country, gumming up the works.

Of those hacks who filled the newspapers with the gaudy lies of sheer propaganda there is no need to speak. They were hallucinations of the bureaucracy whose existence served only to give the hallucinating censors something to measure loyalty by. But, in fact, they were so gross that they made even censors queasy. Paraded on TV and on rostrums on patriotic days, they were a kind of fake folk art, kitsch horror for the forced marches.

My generation, spurred on by the surfacing of books in the libraries of old men, was not a true adversary of the regime. We wanted to escape, not to fight. The older poets we discovered disdained the world: they were symbolists and aesthetes. We felt ourselves to be heirs of the last *fin-de-siècle*, aesthetes who looked for absolutes in the interior, in the mismatched joinings, in the uneven fittings, in the creases, in the crossings of domestic surrealisms with absurd propaganda. We chose to be hermetic and to develop an entire obscure vocabulary of criticism. Unconsciously, we were censoring direct expression, but consciously we were doing a job that had to be done: reconnecting the present with the past. We ignored decades of "social realism" to return insistently to the point of prewar Romanian literature where the tragic break had occurred. We returned to the wounded source determined to join once again the real literature.

Censors did not quite understand the nature of this enterprise. They chose to ignore it because it did not seem to challenge the Party clearly and directly. But our names and books were only *deferred* until the regime needed new enemies. Then we would be reviewed. The year was only 1964, and Romania was but a far country on the border of the Empire.

Such was the situation in the provinces. But in Moscow, at the heart of the Empire, bigger things were happening. Direct criticism of the State, unthinkable to us, was being offered by writers. There were suddenly adversaries, dissidents, *refuseniks* there. The hard police were after them. During the era of loosened Khrushchevian syntax, Aleksandr Solzhenitsyn's *One Day in the Life of Ivan Denisovich* was the first adversary book ever to appear in the Soviet Union. It was an adversary of *the past*. Even so, ideology, which thrives on continuity and does not recognize the past except as a step in a logical progression, was immensely threatened. Even the manuscript of this book inspired fear when it was first presented to Soviet publishers. Many editors refused to look at the bundle of papers, fearing instant contamination. The act of reading had become subversive even in its *potential* state. Khrushchev personally authorized publication, thinking it a useful means of supporting his de-Stalinization speech at the upcoming Party Congress. In other words, where a break with the past was called for, the act of reading became permitted, and an adversary of the past was allowed to speak against it. Of course, Solzhenitsyn was no dummy, and Khrushchev was no ventriloquist. This was a serious miscalculation: the little book opened the floodgates of memory. But then the well-oiled machinery of censorship, which Khrushchev had unplugged for his momentary purposes, was again set running. Not another word about the labor camps was heard in the country where every single citizen had had a relative perish in them.

Far from being the author of a single, simple story, as his friends tried to portray him to the censors, Solzhenitsyn had been writing furiously and secretly for a number of years. One night, some ten years after his powerful book was published, on February 13, 1974, the police arrested him. Solzhenitsyn calculated that he would last only ninety days in jail. He would then commit suicide. Instead of jail, he was put on a plane full of KGB agents and taken to West Germany. The West to which the Soviet State banished him was not to his liking. But it is here that his effectiveness began, because a whole new moral interior surfaced with Solzhenitsyn, namely, the nearly forgotten moral charge of the humanitarian nineteenth century, that clean anti-industrial opposition whose full force we have slowly lost. Outside the Russian borders Solzhenitsyn felt uprooted, like the flying birch set aloft by bearded father Gherasim in the tale "Petrushka and the Talking Forest." Landing in the eye of a media storm, he seemed never to have heard of the twentieth century because, with the exception of about twenty years right at the beginning, the twentieth century never happened in Russia. Those twenty years at the beginning have been written and rewritten by Soviet historians to make it appear that they belonged to the nineteenth century. Virtually no Russians today are capable of fully understanding the teens and the twenties of this century's history. There was little of the twentieth century in Stalin's camps. Hitler's camps were indeed of our century: technical, silent. But in hard-labor Gulag, there reigned only the oppressive darkness of the eighteenth century.

In 1962–63, when Solzhenitsyn emerged from the underground, the brief and excruciating memory of the 1910s and the 1920s also awoke with him. But the Russian modernists were not contemporaries of Solzhenitsyn. He was of Tolstoy's era. In the house of words, time is jumbled up, chewed, and spit out in a different form. If the time machines of the old fairy tales suspended time, the time machines of the State turned it into the pulp of the official present.

Nostalgia for Stalinism, which is sweeping Russia today, is a nostalgia for stability. The Eden of Stalinist innocence where only the murmurs of praise were heard was a slow-paced place for those outside the camps. The inmates of the camps concentrated all the intensity of Soviet society. They rushed at tremendous speed through the entire range of possible human emotions and became either extraordinary in the process, a species of saint like Solzhenitsyn or Eugenia Ginzburg, or ignoble, a brand of succubus. The drama of the camps often took place over staggering distances, hundreds of kilometers on foot through the snow. Human degradation grew geometrically in proportion to the loss of hope. Hunger was the only life of the mind. But then, here is Eugenia Ginzburg in one of the Gulag's deadliest hells, Kolyma, in Siberia, felling trees in the tundra at 49 degrees below zero, reciting the poetry of Blok, Pasternak, Akhmatova. Our casual notions of interior and exterior are transformed here. The outside is indeed vast, but it is, in all its vastness, only the interior of the Soviet prison system. The mind, on the other hand, is occupied by hunger, but there is room for poetry, which is to say infinity, in it. The inside and the outside have switched places. Freedom, synonymous with the outside, is not even desirable to many inmates. An old woman "twice ventured outside the compound during that month, looking for a place of refuge in this incomprehensible free anthill where rations were not doled out every morning and where you didn't have a place of your own on the bunk platform."

In the outside world, the desire to be inside, even under dreadful circumstances, has a strong pull. Vlad Samsonov, a young boy in Vladimir Maximov's *Farewell from Nowhere*, wanders hungry from town to town in Stalin's Russia. He meets a tattered old geezer in a bazaar in central Russia, who offers to trade a pair of felt boots for Vlad's real leather ones. The boy agrees reluctantly, but he is hungry, so he follows the old man for a day and night until they arrive in the dark before a vast, hulking mountain. "What is it? . . . What on earth is that monster?" asks Vlad. "It's Him!" the old man replies with unconcealed pride. "The boss. The old man. Put there to last forever." The boy realizes then that they are standing in front of the gigantic statue of Stalin that straddles the Volga-Don Canal. The old man lives inside the boot in a stinking metal chamber with a goat and piles of junk. Every day, he boasts, he has meat for dinner because the head of the statue is equipped with some sort of death-ray that kills pigeons that attempt to settle on it. In the morning, shod in the inferior felt boots that are too hot, Vlad resumes his wanderings across Russia, until they fall apart.

Stalin's interior was so vast only words could escape it. Not any words. Words charged with power, pointing out even when all there seemed to be was the inside of a metal boot. Says Andrei Synyavsky: "Our problems are completely incomprehensible to those in the West. They cannot understand why it is necessary to destroy someone for writing words, nor why the larger, official body of writers, that vast literary army, cannot utter a word without looking around to make sure that it agrees with the intentions and permitted phraseology of higher authority. Nor why from time to time something goes wrong in the ranks of that army, and someone dashes out and starts shouting furiously as though he thought he were about to turn the world upside down."

After Stalinism, words flowed out, the dams were opened and the pent-up words rushed forth. So loud was the cascade that very few individual voices could be heard above the noise. Khrushchev's Russia is a world made out of talk, a society made out of words. Power comes from the privilege of pronouncing certain strings of unpronounceable initials to make them appear to serve the Ism. Drunk on wine and vodka, the Russians of the 1960s are on a verbal binge. Politics, arts, morals, science, and popular superstitions are all grist for the mill. As soon as a shred of "meaning" appears, it's turned back into words faster than a militiaman can whistle. Official politics, works of art, jail terms, stints in mental hospitals are dependents of verbal growth. The great Russian poets are Yevtushenko and Voznesensky, two loud orators in the tradition of Vladimir Mayakovski who turn large crowds into frenzied mobs the way rock stars do in the West. Gogolian progressions structure the word-sea, inflating everything. The enemy is silence. Once, in the Stalinist Eden, silence was golden. No more. Russia fears silence like the devil. Against it, it is willing to use missiles.

The inflation of the word turned Khrushchev's Russia into a nineteenth-century Russian novel. The dissidents were characters in it. There was Father Solzhenitsyn, suitably Slavophile, a bearded icon hailing from the fourteenth and eighteenth centuries. There was Mother Sakharov, a liberal humanist in the European tradition. There were the Martyred Sons: Mandelstam, Pasternak. The Russian nineteenth century, with its great intellectual debate cut short by Lenin's cadre, emerged whole, like a sunken continent, from the sea of words. From Tolstoy through Gandhi through Martin Luther King, Russian pacifism came full circle with Andrei Amalrik, the human rights activist.

The pathos of talk was intimately tied to drink. In the word-sea there flowed rivers of booze. Drinking is a Russian religion with a complex metaphysic. Benny, the hero of Benedict Erofeev's *Moscow Circles*, sets out on a circular train journey full of hope and vodka. His train companions, also drunk, scream, talk, lie, weep, expostulate, theorize, criticize, and swear. The stations flash by outside without much meaning, facts and figures pile up. At the peak of this orgy of blathering pathos, a sadness begins to insinuate itself. The sadness grows imperceptibly at first, then it engulfs the train. Benny finds himself alone and sad, but still he talks with his soul, with angels, with God, with hallucinations. From Gogol to Dostoevsky to Goncharov, the ineluctable sadness of Russia pours out of Benny. He shouts out a new slogan: "And then we'll have another drink and study, study, study!" Here is one of Benny's cocktails, called "Tears of the Komsomol Girl": lavender water, verbena, forest water, nail varnish, mouthwash, lemonade, vodka. A magic potion from the gris-gris bag of the State.

Of words is the Soviet citizen's fantasy of the West also made. There are mountains of blue jeans there, mile-high neon signs, fast cars, acres of window displays, pulsing neon jukeboxes, loose morals, plentiful spicy things to eat. The hungry Russian's vision of the West resembles exactly the promise the fathers of communism made the workers about the future. Consumerism, it appears, is the goal of communism. The new privileged class of the Party certainly believes this: communism arrived early for them. They drive big American cars. Modern Russia is an homage to Henry Ford, not to Karl Marx. Moscow—the seat of the State, the Ortho-Commie Holy See, is a paternal mesh of personal and political intrigue, a world of spies, drunks, and informers. Class distinctions are rigid between *apparatchiks* and the common people. Only the eternal bohemian and the wandering Jew (often one and the same) move with relative ease in the Red Byzantium. All value systems are based on eatables and wearables. For all that, there is a large, clunky, sentimental yearning here that can be called spiritual, namely, the peculiar Russian idea that the spirit flourishes through suffering, while a surfeit of material objects dulls the consciousness of being. This spiritual masochism is largely pointless because it is so easily granted. Everyone suffers deprivation. There isn't enough material world to reject. The yearning is literary. The spirit resides well in the word, whence it came.

Samizdat was temporarily a way to get around censorship, in order to speak of large, forbidden things. Typed individually and passed from hand to hand, samizdat books were something more than uncensored books. They were free not only of the State but of the literary critical apparatus as well. One can only imagine the dedication of people typing something the size of *The Gulag Archipelago*. Many of these uncensored books found their way to the West where they began to change Western literary taste and climate.

In the Khrushchev era censors never used the word *censorship*. They preferred *rejecting, cutting, banning*. Who were the censors? Vassily Aksyonov provides a partial answer: "Invisible faces, in countless replicas, rank and file of the Party cultural apparatus. People no one knows socially, or even at a distance, people who go home for dinner and are never even *marginally* involved with cultural matters." In other words, middle-class Soviet citizens, people we would describe as setting "community standards." Aksyonov calls the "liberal" Khrushchev era "the soft sands of censorship." In unsoft times, it was thought prudent to eliminate the writer at the same time as the book. Khrushchev's "liberalization" ended effectively with the Prague Spring and the Brezhnev Doctrine, though it lingered on and had another flowering with the Helsinki Accords in the 1970s. A number of dissident groups were formed to observe compliance with the Accords, but their members were imprisoned, committed to mental hospitals, sometimes tortured, and often banished.

The Gorbachev era is making it appear as if decades of censorship have disappeared in a flick of the suddenly relaxed red fist. That's one of the wonders of our media: hailing the alleviation of symptoms as the great healing. But literary liberty is only one of censorship's freed victims. In reality, the removal of overt censorship is now giving birth to the true monsters of suppression, those other deformed beings that had no voice until now: racism, anti-Semitism, panslavism, orthodoxy. These raging beasts will not be tolerated in an empire straining to break into a thousand pieces.

If anything breaks down the Empire, it will not be the intoxicated imaginings of writers in Moscow cafés, but homegrown mobs spurred on by a new generation of pamphleteers as eloquent but not as sophisticated as those of 1905. *Glasnost* is in a race for time with Russia's own awesome past. If Moscow television gets to the people quicker than local pamphlets, Gorbachev's revolution will succeed in keeping the Empire whole. If the cacophony of freed rage in raving print covers Great Russia first, there will be only little fiefdoms left when the paper clouds lift. It will require Siberian armies to piece Russia back together.

Gorbachev is betting the future of his country with our microchips. If we lend him enough, he'll pay us back in advertising opportunities. Together, we will make the world imaginary.

Gorbachev's *glasnost* is not just another attempt at Khrushchevian liberalism. It is a desperate gamble on the possibility that great, healthy market forces will be freed by removing censorship, that consumer goods will be born out of mouthing off. But things are not proceeding as rapidly as the West would like to believe. The editor of the newspaper *Argumenty i Facty* was told to resign after publishing a poll that angered Gorbachev. The major media still belong to the Party. The militia still patrol the streets. And when the forum is truly free, the speaker is usually very hungry.

When the Soviets decided recently to send some of their so-called dissidents on tour to the West, to show that they are free to do so, they had to dust off some of *Khrushchev's* dissidents: Yevgeny Yevtushenko and Andrei Voznesensky. The existence of "show dissidents" points to insecurity in the new Soviet interior. Without outsiders to crush or to exclude from Soviet life, the regime finds it difficult to feel its shape. It needs dissidence the way the police need crime. Real dissidence is hard to manufacture. Hence, Show Dissidence! Nationalism, which is quite emotional, will be trickier to disguise as simple benign pride. Behind the rush to loudly claimed liberties there is yet a powerful illusion-making machine working overtime to make replicas of those genuine yearnings. This illusion-machine is best revealed by the history of exile.

Exile,
a Place

Though eventually he chose to live in the United States, Solzhenitsyn was banished to a place that was not any one country. It was Exile, the place I had been dreaming of ever since hearing that books were not forbidden there. But what I meant by *books* was Adventure. Just as I'd imagined an entire forbidden literature, I was now imagining another, grander unforbidden literature that stretched to the farthest reaches of my imagination. If I gave this sentiment the name *books* it was only because reading them and writing them was what I felt best suited for. The same feeling, however, in various degrees of intensity, thumped in the bosom of my entire generation. Adventure had seized us. Exile was the pure Outside. We could play there to our heart's content without ever being called back in by Mother Country or Father State.

When I left Romania, the idea of being a writer and the idea of being an exile were synonymous. I knew that leaving—or even expressing the desire to do so—would make me an enemy of the State, a political exile. I would lose my Romanian citizenship, and never again be allowed to live in Sibiu. I would never again feed daily on the language that provoked such delirium in my inflamed lyrical self. I would never see my friends again. My sweetheart, Aurelia, would marry someone else and one sad day we would meet, perhaps, in the rain, near the Eiffel Tower, scarred by life, weary and sick, tubercular and disillusioned. Even the very thought of leaving made one a political suspect and a tragic creature. On the other hand, I could barely contain myself because I knew also that I was about to share in a poetic religion. At that time, in 1965, both the very real tragic model of exile (more tragic for those older than I) and the poetic model of vagabonding and exploring came together to form a sort of propeller, a spinning helix, inside of us. On the turbulent spinning of this paradox I would leave my native country, and be aloft until I ran out of fuel, or poetry.

The myth of exile was imbedded archetypally in our culture. I belong to a country whose main export is geniuses. The most famous exile of antiquity, Ovid, was exiled among the ancient Romanians and founded their literature. Since then, in misguided reciprocity, Romanians have been exiling their poets with a single-minded devotion to their beginnings. Obligingly, history hasn't lagged far behind in providing innumerable opportunities. We are powerfully afflicted with a tragic sense of history. To paraphrase Emil Cioran, we have survived by sabotaging history. History belonged, usually, to powerful outsiders whose coming meant only trouble. Time had never done anyone any good, and it had been a lot meaner to those unlucky enough to be situated at the crossroads of East and West. Against history, we developed community through the use of a subtle and ambiguous language that could be heard in one way by the oppressor, in another by your friends. Our weapons of sabotage were ambiguity, humor, paradox, mystery, poetry, song, and magic. When the solar-powered armies marched over us we met with the moon in deep forests. Whether it was the Romans, Turks, Magyars, Goths, or Russians, the only defense of a small people was a massive trust in the miraculous and an active hatred of history.

In 1965 my mind was imbued with the mystical potencies of deracination. I wanted to suffer the way our great exiled poets had suffered, and the way only an adolescent can when he dedicates himself to something greater than himself. It was delicious suffering, made painfully pleasurable by the drumbeats on certain smuggled tapes of Western music, which announced to the world that an entire generation was on the verge of upheaval, no matter where they lived. The decision to be a poet, I told myself, carried with it intrinsically the necessity of exile. "He who writes in Wallachian writes on oatmeal," says the proverb. As for what a poet *does*, the answer was plain: he wanders. From Mioritza to the poems of Ion Barbu, Romanian literature is one long epic of rebirth based on a metaphorical journey. But metaphor and reality are not divisible in our culture. Indeed, our language, in answer to history, revels in the ambiguity.

In the university we whispered the names of our great exiles, which had come to replace those of our smaller national heroes. Among the recent ones, and these were the ones we most felt for, the names of Constantin Brâncusi, Tristan Tzara, Eugène Ionesco, Mircea Eliade, and Emil Cioran sent shivers up our spines.

Brâncusi and Tzara had been poetic exiles, which is to say that they left on their own, fleeing poverty (Brâncusi) or boredom (Tzara). But poverty and boredom are political as well. The difference between the poetic and the political is only three letters. Those letters belong to the State, which can insert them at will, in forms ranging from conscription in the army (a form I, for one, decided to avoid at all cost!) to erasure from memory. Cioran and Eliade, who fled from political persecution by, respectively, Fascists and Communists, were consigned to oblivion for decades, until their reputations became too great to ignore. Fleeing as they did at the height of their creative powers, their exile took on an added sense of the irremediable. For us, the meaning of their exile overshadowed by far the meaning of their creations with which, at the time, we had but a furtive acquaintance.

It occurred to me, of course, that many Romanian intellectuals had fled the idea of what was coming and that I, in many ways, was a product of what came. I was a young poet educated by the new regime and made to absorb a variety of notions that would have appalled my predecessors. But I saw the cultural gap between us as irrelevant. Exile unified us, and, in my mind, it assumed the proportions of a *place*. I wouldn't be just leaving my country—I would be going to a place called Exile. I imagined Exile as a substantial territory, a psychological place of vast dimensions, with distinct boundaries, its own customs, as well as its peculiar tourist attractions. Geographically, this may have been Paris, Rome, New York, Buenos Aires, or San Francisco, but spiritually it began at the borders of the Soviet Empire. This archipelago was inhabited mainly by creative citizens, resembling Plato's Republic of Letters. It was an international Idea-State, the only anarchist system in working order.

The discomforts were seriously outweighed by the heady possibility of emigrating into the company of such men as Mircea Eliade, Emil Cioran, Vladimir Nabokov. As a country, Exile has a far larger pantheon of heroes than, let's say, the United States of America. The actual existence of the place was never in question, and the thought that in order to get there I would have to pass through several *real* countries did not seem terribly important.

The discomforts, including the natural bureaucratic nightmares that accompany expatriation, were of little import to me. The demons that chased me were more poetic than political, though a case can be made for the reverse. You don't have to be a poet to flee the Romanian army (or any army for that matter!), just a sensible person. As a baby dissident, whose early poems had attracted the attention of censors because of their heavy-handed and murky metaphors, I was sure to end up in the precarious position of full-blown dissident. But at the same time, the mid-1960s were a time of cultural opportunities. There was a certain pre-1968 Prague freedom in the air. If no decisive works of social protest came from writers and artists at this time, it wasn't because jail and execution hung over their heads but because self-censorship takes a lot longer to overthrow than State censorship. I was aware of the climate and I could have published, spoken, and possibly agitated as I pleased. But in my heart and mind the myth of exile beckoned. My abilities would remain potential until taken out of the country. This consistent refrain was so much in keeping with the historical thrust of our culture that the present was small by comparison.

When I left Romania, my exhilaration knew no bounds. It took me through the minor disappointment of not being able to stay in Europe, where all my heroes were. I would have liked to stay in Paris but the French took in no refugees. I would have also liked to stay in Italy, but there was no room there either. But I didn't really care where I was going. I applied for visas to several countries, and was accepted by three: Australia, Canada, and the United States. All were English-speaking countries, which would now be my new language. There was no question as to which I would choose: the drumbeats I had heard on the smuggled tapes of

Western music came directly from the United States. That's where the Pied Piper lived.

In so decreeing, my destiny made me party to an unbelievable stroke of luck. An air of freedom was evident everywhere, and a narrow crack had appeared in the solid wall of the political nightmare. I was allowed to go through with all my illusions unchallenged for at least six or seven years. I found my country of exile not in the company of my literal fellow exiles but in the native youth of America. At that time, exile was the status quo. Generations were in exile from each other, thousands of young people roamed the continent in deliberate religious abandon. Exile was part of the popular culture, and its meaning had been expanded to take in anything from an hour of alienation to a summer of slumming in Europe. An entire generation exiled itself for one weekend at a place called Woodstock, forming a "youth nation" that became an exemplary social formation, never before seen in history. *Exile* means "off base" in Latin, but I liked the phonetic associations in English: helix, axis, exit. Whether literal or barely metaphorical, exile is a cluster of paradoxes. I did not find it necessary to maintain the word in a literal state.

The advantages of being a literal exile in a culture obsessed by the myth of it are innumerable. What do Americans see when they look at, a Romanian? Three things: Dracula, Eugène Ionesco, and Nadia Comaneci. In other words, sex, the absurd, and gymnastic ability. These three reflect perfectly both the tone and the content of American life at the near-end of the twentieth century: namely, an obsession with sex, living in a world from which meaning seems to have fled, and the secret belief of everyone that one has to exist gymnastically, continually balancing on the edge of questions—and, if able, doing so gracefully. We coincided transcendentally: I was the answer to big questions. In 1966, only two legs of this symbolic triad

(Ionesco and Dracula) were available to me. Eugène Ionesco, the playwright of the absurd whose work I greatly admired, was only the thinking man's Dracula. With a literary gesture he had torn the veil of realism from the world, and meaning as we knew it was gone. To be bitten by the absurd was the same as being bitten by Dracula: the result was a kind of immortality. The absurd is a potent Balkan brew (first introduced in literary form by Tristan Tzara) which cleanses one of the death-inducing vises of dualism, religion and scruples. If everything, including life and death, is absurd, living forever is a kind of absurd duty, the only activity that flies resolutely in the face of facts. Romania then, as I saw it through others' perspective, was myth-generative. I saw myself enlarging the borders of my quickly mythicizing country. Romania was whatever I said it was.

Dracula was already a figure of some magnitude, having been deified to about the size of Satan's chief of staff. His main function was to bite maidens in their semi-sleep. Since then a relatively minor holiday, Halloween, has increased in importance to the point where it is now overtaking Christmas as the nation's greatest holiday. On Halloween, Dracula is *the* chief deity, and just as Halloween is displacing Christmas, Dracula is replacing Jesus Christ. Only a thin but resilient wall of material consumption still gives Christmas the edge. For me, Dracula was generative to the point of embarrassment. I did resist at first. I was a gloomy young poet for the longest time. He was a queasy product of Hollywood, this Dracula, he sure was. But what a gift! His bite ended being-in-time, reinstated aristocracy and difference, and what a way to meet girls! Even Romania, which for the longest time held its guard up against this purely Western invention, eventually opened its castles to hard-currency-carrying tourists, who were able to groan with expensive terror in the frightening locales (fixed up, incidentally, by a former vice president of Disney!). My own adoption of the myth was only partly opportunistic, however: I recognized in the debased movie version the lines of force that made the historical Dracula, Vlad the Impaler, important to me. Hollywood's Dracula was, granted, a fop and a roué, but he was forced by his sad immortal condition to *invent* continually. Without a prodigious imagination he would not have been able to suffer the tedium of eternal existence. Likewise, the Impaler, propelled by a historical wave, had set himself at the headwaters of the modern world and became its symbolic sluice. Both the real and the imaginary had in common a supreme generative force, and this is the only thing I cared for.

A few years later, there arrived within this sexualized and intoxicated idea a new solution to existence, in the suggestion embodied by Nadia Comaneci, the young gymnast. Nadia's recent defection adds an interesting new dimension to her metaphorical existence: she has now literally vaulted across the Romanian border. She has also leapt so far over our sense of what is proper that she has landed in the tabloids. Her leap into freedom has been completely nonconforming. She has flouted the political and moral authorities of both East and West, a Perfect Ten that has cost her millions of dollars in lost advertising endorsements. Nadia is the spectacular prototype of a new breed of exile from the recently deceased Communist world. She brings her contempt for power to bear on the entire range of it, regardless of political color—an uneasy prospect for cheerleaders of the Eastern European collapse who are, most often, rigid proponents of domestic order.

I did not see at the time that exile was a temporary religion in America. Most of the converts I encountered would soon change faiths and leave the church empty, thereby closing that propitious crack in history. In regarding my exile as a kind of climax of historical process, a peregrination through the "global village," I was making one of the common mistakes of the 1960s. It hadn't been the same for the preceding generation of exiles and it will not be the same for the next generation. I had come at the right time, at a time when my expectations of the West corresponded to the West's expectations of itself. It was a fortunate juncture. I was nineteen years old and so was the world.

For those coming before me, exile had been a dreadful limbo between statelessness and naturalization, a limbo in which one did not tarry in spite of its mythical light. This light shone, if anything, on the distorted faces of the monsters of solitude, loss, and despair. It will be the same, I suspect, for the next refugees. In the 1980s, the Refugee and the Emigré are back in the old spot of misery. Their position will resemble more Nabokov's position in the 1920s and 1930s, of which he wrote, referring to the Germans and Frenchmen he and his family then lived among: "These aborigines were to the mind's eye as flat and transparent as figures cut out of cellophane, and although we used their gadgets, applauded their clowns, picked their roadside plums and apples, no real communication, of the rich human sort so widespread in our midst, existed between us and them." And then, on the next page of *Speak Memory:* "in the course of almost one-fifth of a century spent in Western Europe I have not had, among the sprinkling of Germans and Frenchmen I knew (mostly landladies and literary people), more than two good friends all told."

The opposite was true for me. I did not have, all told, more than two Romanian friends. So open was American culture at the time of my arrival that I was almost instantaneously absorbed by it. Its values, at the time, seemed to be my own. Or rather, my values seemed to be highly regarded by my American contemporaries. I had no way of knowing, as I have said elsewhere, that "America was an uninterrupted anthology of fads chasing each other faster and faster across shorter and shorter time spans."

I must make a distinction here between the kind of expatriate who takes lavishly to a new culture and tries to *pass,* and my own breathless plunge into American life. I was at all times elaborating on my native paradoxes. I saw myself, and I still do, as the ambassador of Romanian poetry, or at least a conveyor of certain Balkanic mysteries of great importance. I did not stop being a Romanian poet when I became an American one. The Romanian language became my covert dimension, a secret engine, like childhood, while American English covered all the aspects of my lived life. In the deep interior I maintained this core of crisis, prayer, high diction—the phrases of drama—in the Romanian language. My daily language, American English, received both fuel and poetry from this core. Eventually they fused, but it took time.

Surrounded by the metaphorical exiles of America, I was doing my best to understand my new culture. Of all aspects of the explosive dynamic of the 1960s, American poetry was most open to experimentation. It was, at the time of my arrival, opening in all directions. The Whitmanic radicals were taking poetry back from the Anglophile academics who had been dominant until then. (In the 1970s the academics came back with a vengeance and poetry was marginalized in the process, until it became no more than a lower-middle-class occupation in the 1980s.)

The American idiom came to me in great gulps, rushes, and explosions. I did not stop to lament my exile. There was nothing to lament, except lack of money, and that wasn't very original. My poetic organ was being fed discoveries at a tremendous pace.

Over two decades, I almost didn't notice that the times had changed. I'd had no time to heed the inklings, so when I finally looked around, I was startled. All around me, the metaphor of exile, so highly regarded in the 1960s, began to take on dark overtones and a new nationalism was on the loose. The wholesale abandonment of poetic religions had begun amid a new search for roots, identity, and, ultimately, nationalism. In the 1970s "ethnics" began to replace "aliens." In the cities, "ethnic fairs" appeared, at which curiously costumed crypto-peasants sold fly-covered, meat-filled lumps of various sorts. At the same time, the Immigration Department's power to make new Americans took on new ideological rigidity. The influx of peoples from Latin America, Asia, and Africa led to new calls for restrictions. Racism and xenophobia began to creep into daily life. My own battle with the Immigration and Naturalization Bureau was prolonged and epic, but I had little taste for it. I tried to be neither an "ethnic" nor a "minority," but an aristocrat, a poet.

My exile appeared to me, for the first time, in a historical light. Times of great freedom breed metaphorical exiles, while times of repression breed literal exiles. I had been granted a temporary reprieve from the reality of my exile by the ascendance of the myth. This contact with reality did not change my belief in the therapeutic value of my wandering. Metaphorical exiles who shed their allegiance to the myth of exile also forfeit their claim to poetry. This is a tragic position because they will never be natives again either: the prodigal son is always an oddity. But their desertion left me in a strange position. I found myself in a place that had emptied itself in a few years like a Mexican town at siesta time.

This is when the thought of my literal fellow exiles began to dawn on me and I made a mad dash for a belated connection. Exile for them was indeed a unifying experience, but not as I first thought. It was held together not by its heroes but by quixotic dignity and pain. The contacts among its illustrious citizens were sporadic and fraught with long silences. It was in those silences that the "story" of exile unfolded. It was as if each exile was an unfinished sentence, a phrase impossible to understand without the native text from which it had been plucked. I learned to read ellipses. Exile was a literal, not a metaphorical, condition for most humans, including the ones I had exalted, and attitudes toward the myth of exile and its resulting propaganda varied not only from generation to generation but from country to country. The unity was in an outraged sense of betrayal by history.

My position was, once again, odd. I did not feel separated from the culture of my native country in a painful way. The realization, of course, that I might never be able to return caused a certain amount of anguish; occasionally, a peculiar nostalgia that Romanians call *dor* would seize me with a light of times and places reachable only in memory. If Ovid was our first poet, then his "Tristia" ("The Sorrows"), in which he laments his exile, is our first poem. But while enacting the sorrows of my poet, I was simply carrying on the concerns of my culture with a different set of tools. The big question for me was the necessity of my culture in the larger scheme of things. The only thing I feared was obsolescence. I had ample reasons to believe, however, that my concerns, far from being obsolete, answered to something calling urgently from inside my new world. I was in love with the myth of exile and I was disappointed with its sudden recession in the 1970s. About history I did not feel one way or another and this put me, I guess, in exile from my fellow exiles.

I don't want to minimize the realities of expatriation by referring so much to the myth, which lies, finally, in a gray area and can be claimed by anyone wishing to put some distance between himself and society. But I have little choice. The reality of my exile has, so far, been less important to me than the myth.

In modern times the myth of exile has conquered the West. If an image were to be invented as the proper icon of the beginning of these times, it would have to be a photograph of Lenin and Tristan Tzara playing chess in a Zurich café in 1916. The two exiles often met for that purpose, but there is no record of their conversations. One imagines two slightly bored onlookers watching over the shoulders of the two refugees with expressions of superior indulgence for the obviously amateurish quality of the game. But the snobbish spectators would be terribly wrong. It is a great game, this game between politics and poetics, and it goes on still.

Tristan Tzara, the exiled Romanian Jew, is the founder of the Dada movement and the embodiment of the poetic exile. From the stage of Cabaret Voltaire in Zurich, a concentric negation rippled through the capitals of Europe, bringing with it a virulently antimilitaristic, antinationalist, and antibourgeois wind. It tore through the flimsy sails of reason and it revealed the grotesque shape of the doombound vessel carrying Europe. From Zurich to Berlin to Paris to Vienna, the unnaturally optimistic masks of the bourgeoisie were suddenly torn, leaving the rubicund faces exposed to the gruesome laughter of Dada. Our century's artistic self begins in the antiauthoritarian Dada explosion. It was an international movement of exiles and, by the end of World War I, it had changed us forever. The eighteenth-century view of ourselves as creatures of reason fell resoundingly apart. From the debris, man, creature of the irrational, stepped forth. Or should we say stepped aside: in the vacated center of the debris, the machine stepped in. In fact, reasonable man and implacable machine neatly changed places. Henceforth, a marginal human will forever try to reclaim the place the machine occupies.

The Dadaists were regarded with more suspicion than the revolutionary Russians by the Swiss authorities. Hans

Richter, in his book, *Dada: Art and Anti-Art,* says: "Diagonally opposite, at No. 12 Spiegelgasse, the same narrow thoroughfare in which the Cabaret Voltaire mounted its nightly orgies of singing, poetry and dancing, lived Lenin. Radek, Lenin and Zinoviev were allowed complete liberty. It seemed to me that the Swiss authorities were much more suspicious of the Dadaists, who were after all capable of perpetrating some new enormity at any moment, than of these quiet, studious Russians."

Dada, by its exacerbation of individual freedom, lent a sudden vitality to the myth of exile. Word-weary and word-profligate, Dada finished the dominion of words in the West. Lenin's move was to attach a bomb to the word. Tzara's was to defuse whatever still pertained of terror to it. Hundreds of artists and writers in the West began going into exile on an unprecedented scale. The great cities—Paris, Vienna, Berlin, London—became exile capitals. Modern American literature was the work of Paris exiles. It was the same for British literature. Terry Eagleton writes: "If it is agreed that the seven most significant writers of twentieth-century English literature have been a Pole, three Americans, two Irishmen and an Englishman, then it might also be agreed that the paradox is odd enough to warrant analysis."

Lenin, too, strengthened the myth of exile in his own fashion. After the success of the Bolshevik Revolution, the country's entire intelligentsia emigrated to the West. There was no going back for these exiles, however, and this was a major difference between them and the wandering Westerners. The difference was of tragic dimension and many exiled Russian intellectuals did not recover. They were lost amid futile hopes of return, and often they suffocated in the excessive cultural demands of their own milieu. The history of the Romanian intellectual community in Paris after World War II parallels the Russian situation in many respects. But unlike the Romanians, for whom the futility of belonging to the temporal had been deeply written in their almost Oriental view of fate, the Russians did not have good weapons to "sabotage history," in Cioran's phrase. The curse of a sometimes successful history is to foster the illusion that things will get better.

Through the offices of both poetic and political exiles, the West, between the two world wars, became a vast airport of cultural misfits. Surrealism, which took its energy from Dada and its cultural stand from the psychology of the unconscious, internationalized Western thought to a new level. The unconscious, as proposed by Freud and adopted by the Surrealists, was an alternative to nationalism: it was universal, preverbal, and constant.

The reaction in the making was, of course, fascism. A tremendous search for a redefinition of the native began in Europe, and the attack on the "outsider" began naturally with the Jews, a visible race of exiles par excellence.

After World War II, when fascism failed to stem the tide and, on the contrary, compounded the phenomenon by the deracination of millions of people, the myth of exile continued undaunted.

Russian communism also perceived the internationalizing of culture as a threat and, after the war, the conquered Eastern European countries were forced to acquiesce in a tragic replay of the aftermath of the October revolution. In a few years, their best minds were in exile. Ironically, communism began as an international movement that exhibited, at least in the beginning, the same nihilistic and utopian features that some artistic avant-gardes did. Those ideas, alas, were the first to go with the advent of real power. Power, in whatever form, purges itself first of idealism, then of the minds that still harbor it, and then of anything outside itself. Writers sympathetic to socialism and communism felt the brunt of the State sooner and quicker than avowed adversaries. Ironically, in the Communist-nationalist fiefdom of Romania, the old fascist nationalists (those who didn't die in prison) were brought out of their ratholes by Ceauşescu to aid in the new enterprises of racial hatred, cultural genocide, and police terror. Their expertise was useful.

My own slice of postwar history began under the aegis of existentialism, which popularized "alienation," "the outsider," and "the exile" as the main symbols of the contemporary human condition. This, I wanted to believe, was the end of nationalism.

The West, which was the recipient of this wealth of alien talent, found its national traditionalisms powerfully challenged and, finally, defeated. Whether voluntary, involuntary, missionary, political, or metaphorical, the exile has always been directly in conflict with the native. Generally, it has been a battle over perspective. The exile has access to the totality of the foreign culture because he is not bound by regional or class views. Having lost the regional and class ties of his own culture, he has arrived Outside, where only two options present themselves: a futile effort to recreate the old ties in the new context, or a complete remaking that involves the abandonment of the old and the widest possible perspective on the new. Most émigrés opt for one or the other (unsatisfactory solutions both), but then there are those who settle for nothing less than the overthrow of the entire world system that makes such massive dislocation possible. The Dadaists were the first moderns to glimpse the possibility of a total revolt leading to a pure Outside, but exile itself is conducive to the creation of dangerous organic revolutionaries of the same persuasion. Traditionally, exiles have confined themselves to a few Western capitals but from there their influence has spread concentrically because these capitals are the centers of all Western culture.

The native holds, of necessity, a historical position

against the exile's confirmed metaphysic. The metaphysic of exile views the human condition as a series of tragic events. There was a Fall, and man was in exile. This Fall, repeated by every religion and mythology on earth, proves that man began his existence on earth as an exile. Leaving the womb compounds the original Fall with a new sense of estrangement. Life consists, it seems, in a variety of ways of *not being at home.* Consciousness itself is in exile from biology. History is an exile from paradise. A "home" as such can exist only in a temporal perspective, which is illusory and limited to the indulgence of history. History is rarely indulgent. It ruthlessly displaces people and will continue to do so.

The meeting of a cruel history with a dynamic metaphysic defined the nomad until very recently. To the settled peoples of the world, the nomad was pure evil, the Outsider a synonym for Bad. A scholar of myth, Felicitas D. Goodman, posits the opposition in this way: "The tiller is in constant conflict with 'bad' plants, animals and people that try to intrude into his fields, barns and village. He has an intense feeling of being protected 'within,' while trying to keep the 'outside,' that which is alien and dangerous, both human and alternate reality agencies, from penetrating. In agriculturalist tradition, the inside-outside, that is, the good–bad distinction is transposed also into the hereafter, so that there is a heaven and a hell, and a host of *very good* and *abysmally evil* beings." Being a homeless creature of hell, an outsider, and a nomad, I was in a magical position, attested to by the entire arsenal of human thought.

Throughout time whole races have gone into exile and, while their reasons are open to discussion, they have made the metaphor available on an unimaginable scale. The Mongol hordes found the limitations of geography unendurable. The Jews had a quarrel with God, and have since held their conversations with Him wherever they could, in whatever places they found themselves. Gypsies found a religion in mobility and an opportunity to mock the native obsession with order. As *en masse* abandonment of place, exile is an alternative human organization. The State is the organization of the static, Exile the organization of movement. Until recently nomad life proliferated outside the borders of empires. Today it is being eliminated by the gods of technology who are efficiently accomplishing what religion was patently unable to for thousands of years. Imagination, the nomad's sole possession, is under fire in our time. And what of literature, its child? Exile and impermanence are there at the beginning of literature. Oral traditions speak relentlessly of journeys. Heroes leave and seldom return. If they do, it is under magical circumstances, in an atemporal fashion, with the aid of the gods. All journeys begin in the adversities of history and end through the benevolence of the divine. Homer wandered and sang of other wanderers. We are all exiles if only because, by virtue of His never having left the womb, God is the only native.

It was my mistake, when arriving in America in the 1960s, to view the popularity of the myth of exile as "the end of history." It had simply been a time of triumph for the metaphor through the graces of modern technology. The paradox of the condition remains untouched.

Twentieth-century poets, with Homer, Dante, and the *trovadors* in back of them, have viewed exile therapeutically. Freedom of the spirit was available only by leaving home. They answered the siren call of the Elsewhere for many reasons, but mainly because they were not able to breathe at home. The deep breath is the breath of travel, of speed, of horseback, of movement. The individual "I" had to explode its well-defined limits. "I is another" (*Je est un autre*), said Rimbaud. "My mind grew too big for the Balkans," said Tzara. The mind is a rapacious beast whose appetites outgrow geography. Freedom is a greedy appetite of the mind, and both "time" and "geography" conspire against it, undernourish and frustrate it. This hunger is at the core of poetic exile, its need to establish an atemporal, aspacial identity capable of taking on all the temporalities and localities of its habitations. This identity affirms whatever is true-in-motion, and is simultaneously an "escape" and a "remaking," both religious metaphors. "In the clear night of noon, we proffer more than one new/Proposition on the essence of being," sings St. John Perse.

Freed of the tribe's conventions, the poet is free to express the critical dictates of his instant nomad passage. A history by "flash" flares in his wake. In the wealth of new selves available to him in a new place, he can choose to be historical or he can disappear entirely. Yet he can participate in revolutionary epochs only when individual expression is still at a high premium. If a crowd has gathered to watch, he will have to disappear. Judging from postrevolutionary and postdisappearance accounts, the poet who insists too long on his revolutionary or exilic role will become either a figure of ridicule like Casanova or a martyr like Mayakovski. Changing exiles becomes, like Mao's permanent revolution, a declaration of faith but also a means of saving one's hide or soul. History, of course, does poets no favors, but the instinct for renewal is above all ideological infatuation and may survive both historical adversity and posthistorical diminishing—and may even grant immunity from history. Myth is capable of such dispensation.

Outside the world of myth and of the poet-artists who are part of it lie the worlds of political exiles and those of refugees of every shade and persuasion. There are millions of exiled victims of recent history whose true feelings are not known. Do they secretly believe that the shores of Exile are the barbaric provinces, the places where their culture is *not*? And if so, is their exile a constant meditation on their culture? Are they the subjects of a paralyzing nostalgia? Do they suffer from an implacable sadness that will not ease for generations? Since there are many ways of perceiving the condition, and very few pure examples of it, only exiled writers can answer these questions and they may be the worst reporters. Perhaps the truly unhappy will never be heard. But if they learn to speak, they will be infected by the joy of being Outside, and they will be unhappy no longer. The speech that makes it well destroys what it is about.

PART
THREE

The New Map

A new map of the world is in the making. Countries of memory that were once real countries again make their appearance: once erased from the map, they first reappear as ghost images, quickly draw substance to themselves, and soon are undeniably here. Czeslaw Milosz's long-gone Lithuania appeared from the fog of his *Issa Valley* and is now part of our world. A country named Masuria, between Poland and Germany, came out of a novel by Siegfried Lenz. Isaac Bashevis Singer's Poland took its place on the map a few hovering ghostly inches above today's Poland. Alive in the memories of these writers, the erased countries of the world emerge into the twentieth century to finish their unfinished destinies. Somehow all strains will be played out, and those of murdered nations are no exceptions. They emerge and emerge until all is spent, tried out, consumed. This is the geography of the victims of history returning via the imagination to possess the present. This map shows no distinction between reality and dream: it's drawn to scale.

There are also real countries on the new map, countries where history has been so patently falsified that only the most monumental and radical rewriting, leading to a renaming, will restore them. In these places writers must become quixotic Atlases. Solzhenitsyn's Russia is one of these. He has single-handedly blocked in the vast outline of the true forbidden shape of his country, daring his contemporaries to contribute the details. It was an immense act of recreation, possible only in the vast vacuum of Russia where truth had been missing for so long that a man standing even at a modest height could take in wide horizons.

There are still other countries on the new map, countries of both memory and some sort of geographical reality, whose mythic description is the only true one. Gabriel Garcia Marquez's Colombia-become-Macondo is one of these. The mythical description is so infinitely superior to the provincial gangsterism of the real place that one has no qualms in calling for the abolishing and renaming of Colombia. The overthrow of the real is the chief product of the citizens of Exile.

The Eastern/Central Europeans and the Latin Americans work, of course, from different premises and are under different exigencies to create. And the ex-citizens of completely disappeared countries labor under other orders yet. One can sense that the emergence of a Terra of the imagination will be both awesome and terrible to behold. One may even indulge in some prenostalgia for our present Terra. The real wars that used to change the geography of the world in the ages of hard materials are now being waged psychically in this age of information. The creative rethink-

ing of the world is not a benign operation. The recreated
world emerges *everywhere* at once outside the borders of its
various loci. Milosz's Lithuania of childhood exists only in
his book, no matter what real country may claim our
momentary attention.

In this age of information, the myths of the outsiders are
the real facts, while the facts of the insiders are obscure
fictions. In the West, where technology is dissolving various
nationalisms, there is a certain greed—nostalgia perhaps—
for the seeming integrity of national myths, but only in their
fictionalized, aestheticized form. National battles are being
waged on several levels of reality today: In the West, a tele-
vision-projected cosmopolitan global village with less and
less distinctive local features, is awash in nostalgia for
difference, ethnicity, regionalism. The same global instru-
ment, TV, is bringing us news of the very real struggles for
national identity inside the Soviet Empire, struggles that, in
addition to demanding the recovery of the past, aim also for
a higher standard of living, one that will, eventually, bring
its citizens into the featureless global village of the West.
Recently, in Romania, the mad dictator was bulldozing the
ancient villages and moving the peasants into cement cu-
bicles in 1950s-style buildings on the edges of mammoth
industrial cities. Between the media mirage in the West and
the leveling-by-terror in the East play all the fictions of
"homeland." Preeminent among these are the literally fictional visions of exiled writers.

Milosz's Lithuania is a country of childhood, of history,
and of myth. Its reality is generated by the power of childhood to (mis)understand a religious idea. The awesome
responsibility of being at once preserver and author of his
country is offset by the child's potential for committing an
enormity at any given moment. Milosz is kin to the earliest
chroniclers of history. The old chroniclers wrote things

down at the beginning of history in order to record the deeds of their princes and the beliefs of their tribe. Theirs was a language of facts but also of myth, a poetic language out of which came all later literature. The freshness of *illo tempore* still breathes on their words, imbuing them with the fecundity of all beginnings. Hieronymus Surkont, an ancestor of Thomas, the narrator of *Issa Valley*, is a writer/nation builder. His words invent the future and the people. Young Thomas comes at the end of the history of his people, a few dim moments before the end of Lithuania. He chronicles the end of the nation. He reconstructs his country from a childhood oddly placed in an odd country in an odd century at an ill-omened crossroads of history. A lonely child, an aristocrat who speaks Polish, the careful observer of birds and plants is given access to spirits and demons, pre-Catholic *locus genii* who teach the infinite sorrow of the toppling of the ancient magical order to give way to the twentieth century. Alternating between loneliness and foreign values, between myth and history, Thomas bends in on himself like a question mark punctuating a riddle only he will be able to answer—which he does, by reinventing Lithuania. Between the ancient scribes of the beginning and the exiled poet of the end stretches the whole cruel mindlessness of time. As the world of the insistent mythic particular disappears, the only human authorities will be these Milosz-like stubborn eschatologists with the curled lip, which is to say all of us.

For Milosz, a European humanist, thinking is a natural activity, like walking. And the mind is his home, a home both more durable and more useful than the succession of homes he has had since breaking with Poland in 1951. Living at the edge of the Western world, in the Berkeley of the 1960s, Milosz found the conflicts of our age in full, prototypical bloom. A perfect place to plant a country. If the

early waves of immigrants came here to forget the old world, some of the later ones came to remember it. Not mechanical remembrance, but recreation based on the questions posed by the new. Central to this recreation is the preservation of childhood, that cult of inspiration whose essence is composed of questions. Writing in 1969, Milosz notes of the present age that "never has the division between man as a unique creature and man as a cipher, the co-creator of the unintended, been so clear-cut, and perhaps it was the calling of America, Europe's illegitimate child, to compose a parable of universal significance."

A curious sentence, full of odd phrases. What does Milosz mean? "Illegitimate child" should be ironic. It isn't. Milosz writes like a statesman and is intent on the gravity of his sentence. The only legitimate child is the one that witnessed the destruction of Lithuania. Milosz will not allow anyone or anything else the distinction of childhood. Childhood to Milosz is too serious to be left to innocents such as he perceives Americans to be. "Man as a unique creature" is for Milosz religious man, the creature capable of transcendence, worship, meaning, and virtue. "The co-creator of the unintended" refers to man as innocent spawner of machines, the collective double, the mass-man (Everyman), the technological naïf, the conformist. In California, he finds the two locked in mortal combat. He traces the sources of the combat to the Europe he has left behind. At the same time he follows unsentimentally the raging of that conflict within himself. He finds that he came to America for the same reason the countless masses of desperate, hungry Europeans came in the nineteenth century. The European nineteenth century of ideas, music, and literature camouflaged and ended up excluding the other nineteenth century of brutal industrialization, famine, and uprootedness. The "illegitimate children" of Europe came here from that other century, leaving Europe stranded among its own impossible intellectual demands, demands that soon would lead to two world wars and the slaughter of millions.

In 1969 in Berkeley, Milosz had ample material for reflection. He uses the phenomena of the time curiously, as if the drama of particulars existed solely to highlight his inner conflict, a conflict made of ideas clashing in him since the beginning. The details of his existence in exile are stage lights that illuminate the various aspects of the reconstruction of Lithuania *ex nihilo*. Ideas are real to him, attaining in his hands the concrete substance of building materials. More solid than history or momentary perception, the child's inspired logic makes the virtual manifest. He sees the industrial Moloch of America (he uses Allen Ginsberg's word) as a Second Nature, more terrifying than the first must have been to the original settlers. This Second Nature is a collective creation we have made with our detached doubles from which issue our instructions and specifications (even as to the shape of body and style of thinking) through the mass media. The mechanical rape of nature proceeds on the same scale as the chilling mindlessness of a nature devoid of meaning. The contradictions surrounding him seem to Milosz to demand a clear choice. Oriental fatalism is not for him. Faced with a choice between two orders of mindlessness, one natural, the other mechanical, he chooses to look for meaning, even if it means reinventing it *ex nihilo* like Lithuania. "In modern times the great metaphysical operation has been the attempt to invest history with meaning. That is, we, as foreigners, intruders, face a world that knows neither good nor evil; so let our labyrinth but increase, let our law, born of the challenge we hurl at the world in the name of what should be, be established."

Where does Milosz speak from? What does the place his world springs from look like? Geographically it is no more than a riverbank on which a child lies dreaming. The child is open: through him streams the magical substance of a myth to which the facts of the world will add nothing. When he is wrenched from that riverbank, he will wander the world, forcing it to conform to the dimensions of that long-ago dream. For the grownup wrenched from this child, the actual world—and the humans in it—will be mere shadows projected on the screen of the original myth. It is not a comforting thought. Milosz in his mythical mission is not an angel of mercy. Nor is he a lover of particular humans or an appreciator of physical beauty. His mission is to destroy the specificity of the unmediated moment in order to enlist its energy to the cause of myth.

Milosz's contemporary, Witold Gombrowicz, provides a tonic antidote to Milosz's fundamental operation. An earlier exile, Gombrowicz left his native Poland in 1939 for Argentina, where he lived in poverty, producing astonishing fiction and drama in Polish. Three of his novels, *Cosmos, Pornografia,* and *Ferdydurke,* were published by Grove Press in the United States in 1967. His play *The Marriage* was produced and well received in Europe. For all that, he has remained outside the canon of internationally recognized great writers from Eastern Europe. Czeslaw Milosz, whom Gombrowicz, with some pointed reservations, admired, has gone on to garner a Nobel Prize and the focused attention of the West. The difference between them is instructive. Milosz has placed himself at the center of the pitched battles of history, wrestling large current issues in a language that allows for the coexistence of ideological programs with his mystical mission. He writes beautifully, with a literary jurist's lofty concision. He bristles with grave ideas. One would turn away if he did not, as Gombrowicz observed, "quicken our pulse." Milosz's quickening is of the kind that comes with the fear, awe, and nostalgia of myth. Gombrowicz also quickens the pulse, but his is the affirmative sexual quickening of hope. Human beings in Gombrowicz's world are in urgent need of a complete remaking precisely because large issues have put them outside of themselves. Gombrowicz demystifies himself and the world he lives in with relentless and inspired passion. Humans are more important than ideology; play is more important than duty. "The world has become mortally and stupidly serious and our truths, which are denied play, bore themselves and through their vengeance bore us." This is a profound statement in a century that has seen Fascism, Communism, and the Atomic Bomb, all deadly serious things connected to all the other deadly serious things, including Literature with a capital L. Gombrowicz's disdain for high art is uncompromising. "The West has remained faithful to absolute value and still believes in art. Where they see a man kneeling before Bach's music, I see people who force each other to genuflect and feel delight and admiration."

Gombrowicz heals me instead of enlisting me and is thus much closer to my generation than Milosz, whose uncompromising metaphysic demands clear distinctions between good and bad, between inside and outside. Gombrowicz restores the dignity of the human gesture against the claims of ideas, and in so doing he pours balm over my fearful modern self. He serves up a powerful antidote against the poison of politics and, more important, provides a manner of thinking that liberates. Volume One of his *Diary* covers the years between 1953 and 1956, the peak years of the Cold War. It is heartwarming to hear Gombrowicz at this precise dark moment, opposing ideological polarization. To Milosz's bleak vision of demon communism in *The Seizure of Power*, Gombrowicz replies: "Wouldn't it be more in keeping with history and with our knowledge of man and the world if you treated the world from behind the curtain not as a new, incredible, and demonic world but as a devastation and distortion of a normal world?" This is an incalculably useful attitude, particularly for my generation of postwar exiles, who have been caught in the vise grip of our predecessors' polarized rhetoric. Gombrowicz, as he does in so many different areas, liberates us from both our expressive difficulty and the imperatives of propaganda. We who were raised behind the curtain know for a fact that we were not raised by demons. But it takes someone like Gombrowicz, who had no first-hand experience of the Communist era, to let us out of the magnificent but oppressive cages that Solzhenitsyn and Milosz have built for us. Anticipating the Solidarity movement by three decades, he warns the Catholic Church not to become solely a force for resisting, or "the pistol with which we would like to shoot Karl Marx."

Gombrowicz provides a way out of the desperate intellectualism of postwar exiles with a deadly serious humor. He sets more seemingly self-evident pieties on their heads than a dozen philosophers could, with the possible exception of Nietzsche, to whose "gay science" he fully subscribes. In addition to the well-placed volleys against art and ideology, we are present at the efforts of a unique intelligence to understand itself. Gombrowicz is as merciless with his own betrayals as he is with those of the world. He discusses his sexuality with a sense of wonder, and marvels constantly at his "childishness," which is sometimes a glorious value, at others a great sorrow. "Playing" is the key to the transformation of human beings, and Gombrowicz plays with the concentration and seriousness that children bring to it, even—or especially—when his toys are big: his own self, Poland, Argentina, communism, art. When he is done spinning them around on the floor of the actuality he acutely inhabits, he has exposed, revealed, humanized them: they have become manageable—and, by extension, our future does not seem so threatening anymore. His spirit marks the end of a certain theoretical rigidity, and is the beginning of my generation's active new world view.

I B. Singer's Poland cannot be located on any map either, although a place with a similar name has taken its place. The dybbuks, angels, and plain humans of Singer's universe are illuminated with a profound, mysterious light by the impending tragedy of the Holocaust. Everything is for the last time: the world will never again be the same. But for now, "So long as Hitler didn't attack, so long as no revolution or pogrom erupted, each day was a gift from God." During this lull, which is a gift of time, the bittersweet, superstitious, mystical Jews of Warsaw go on with their daily lives. These ghetto Jews— Talmudists, small tradesmen, young Socialists, penniless writers, and street riffraff—live intact in Singer's prose, ready to spring from the pages of the book which *is* the world, as Singer and the Talmudists know. You can read backwards and still find everyone alive in the book, just as you knew them. Death doesn't exist except as ignorance, as illiteracy. What these people, in the twilight of another age, are discussing is what still concerns us today. Death gives them an intensity we do not have, it is true, but we live through theirs. We are no farther along in our battles against fanaticism and automatism.

One has only to look at Roman Vishniak's photographs in *A Vanished World* to see what stuff that world was made from. Vishniak, using hidden cameras, braving incredible dangers, crossed and recrossed the borders of Poland, Hungary, Romania, and Carpathian Lithuania in Czechoslovakia to take pictures of Jews. The years were 1936 to 1938, just before the world went mad. Vishniak roamed the ghettos and the shtetls, and secretly recorded that vanishing world. He took 16,000 pictures. Of those, 2,000 survive. He smuggled some of the negatives, sewn into the lining of his coat, out of Europe to America. If, as the Kabalah says, there are seventy-five righteous men on whose shoulders the world rests, there are 180 photographs in this book in which a vanished world lives on. It is difficult to look at these images. Is it possible to keep in mind at the same time something that is and something that isn't? That something was, and then is no more—not in the natural course of time, but almost immediately after the pictures were taken? These people went to their deaths almost exactly as we see them: in the puzzle of their childhood, in the flower of their youth, in the perplexity of their old age. We see them all: scholars argue through the gray slush of Europe; wide-eyed children look to their teachers in amazement, the Torah open in front of them; sages, rabbis, Zaddiks, Hassids in flapping black vestments and wide-brimmed hats pass like clouds through the streets, books under their arms. Everywhere there are children, their eyes filled with questions we cannot answer. There is suffering, worry, joy, love, pleasure. Says Elie Weisel, about Vishniak: "He loves them because the world they lived in did not, and because death has already marked them for its own—death and oblivion as well."

The European Jews of 1935 to 1938, my mother's cousins and sisters, already had been marked for destruction. As the world was tensing for war and Hitler's ovens began slowly warming, Vishniak's mission was a sacred one. Like a modern-day prophet, he writes a lamentation in the language of images, the idiom of the twentieth century. Here is Nat Gutman, a porter in the Jewish ghetto of Warsaw. He radiates a defiant dignity. The carrying of loads is the only job permitted Jews in Poland. Another porter, in addition to other burdens, pulls a cart containing his father, who lost his legs in a Russian pogrom thirty years before. The old man has a wise and painful smile. Even the children know. Here is little Sara, who cannot leave her bed all winter because she does not have any clothes. Her big, black eyes look directly into ours. Where, she asks, is the rest of my life? Above her bed, her father has painted some flowers. They are the only flowers she knows.

Vishniak's other children, from Seder scholars to street ragamuffins, share a seriousness and understanding beyond their years. In the crumbling innards of the old Polish cities, the threadbare objects of poverty glow with a life of their own. Here is a peddler with two customers, bent over a coat, carefully examining the fabric. There is an incredible *materiality* in this coat, paradoxically suggesting its opposite: spirituality. When that coat falls apart, the whole world will go with it. Soon, human beings will also become things, to be discarded and junked. Two sisters are eating soup, or rather they are looking dreamily past their soup at something. Time has slowed down so much, it is not soup that they seem to be eating, but time itself. As in a medieval fairy tale, the end of the soup may mean the end of time. Each swallow is a minute, each spoonful an hour. The hidden camera has captured another hidden mechanism, that of time. A little girl stands bewildered before her teacher. She does not know the answer to the question the teacher has just asked her: "What is the biggest city in the world?" Vishniak says: "I would have helped the girl but I didn't know the answer either." This happened in Warsaw, in 1938.

Vishniak's people inhabit Singer's vanished Poland.

Singer's Jews love to make jokes but life itself is no joking matter to them. By the mid-1960s, however, life in Eastern Europe had become a joke. The quintessential form of truth telling in those countries had become the joke. In addition to the joke's time-honored parabolic, satirical, and pedagogical functions, there was an existential/eschatological dimension that included everything. The Joke metamorphosed to become total. The inhabitants of the interior of the Joke reflected it in myriad ways. They laughed to death, and others laughed and died watching them. Milan Kundera's novel *The Joke* follows the Joke in one of its more familiar but least discussed guises: simulation of the real. Everything in mid-1960s Prague was a simulation. Folkloric "ensembles" imitate folklore. Communist Party members imitate Western capitalist fashions. Young Czech kids imitate what they imagine to be young American kids. Imitation extends to emotional life, where everyone is caught in a whirl of simulation of feelings. The lies have become so generalized it is impossible to remember the truth. The truth, of course, has been relativized by earlier imitations and is now without expression.

For Kundera the real and the real-sounding are complete and perfect opposites. But unlike some Westerners he believes that a discerning, or merely awake, person is capable of telling the difference. Things that resemble each other superficially can be substituted for one another only so long as we sleep. And we sleep, in the East as in the West. In the East, imitation is more abstract, manifesting mostly in formulaic declarations of faith. In the West, imitation is done in plastic. Part of one's ability to distinguish between simulacra is having a knack for metaphors that matter. Kundera's "laughter and forgetting," "lightness and heaviness" are of this order. Finding and staying with crucial metaphors is essential. The metaphor is both shelter and healer. Using "laughter and forgetting," Kundera was able to create a phenomenal critique of memory that held within it, amazingly, the possibility of mnemonic demiurgy. He pointed to the exact places in his memory where the generative, creative urge is located, thus freeing himself (and us) from piousness and the fear of the present. He invents a mnemo-erogeny. Having come to artistic maturity about the time of the Prague Spring in 1968, and then gone into exile in the 1970s, Kundera had to remake himself in order to continue. In order to write he had to remember, but in order to be he had to forget. What to forget and what to remember? It is a tension peculiar to exile, but it has vast importance beyond it. In the West we are faced with the catastrophic loss of memory brought about by industreality. We are compelled to forget even the immediate past by the collage style of the mass media. Living in a continual forgetting (an active act), we can only face forward, in a kind of parody of the Communist goal which always bids the masses to step "forward." Progress is the act of forgetting. In the East, where progress is the State god, history has been rewritten to fit its demands, so remembering is a point of honor. How Eastern Europeans remember becomes an essential tool in our human remodeling kit. But what is the point (and indeed, the strength) of that honor when the honorable person doesn't live there anymore but here, where forgetting is such sweet narcotic?

Kundera remembers, as few Western writers do, the original purpose of the art: to discover the hidden sources of being in our time. Here in the West, we have been mired in questions of ethics (Should fiction be moral?) versus aesthetics (Should a book answer only to itself?). Kundera disregards that as nonsense. The main thing, he says, is the intelligent investigation of the world. What really matters is what we really know. When he reminds us of our ontological purpose, he renews us. His characters are ruled by varying quantities of lightness or weight, a uniquely contemporary condition. "Lightness" is the physical equivalent of forgetting. But it serves a spiritual end as well. It is necessary if the organism is to survive. There is a magnificent analysis here of betrayal as a positive notion, an act of assertion and freedom. What for the artists is an escape is for society a betrayal. "My enemy isn't Communism," says Sabina, the artist-heroine of *The Unbearable Lightness of Being*, "but kitsch!" Precisely. Western liberalism, for instance, is pure kitsch. Her liberal Swiss lover, Franz, who hears the heroic strains of the Grand March in his heart, views Sabina symbolically as some kind of Gulag creature from the Revisionist East. In his heart of hearts he still believes in the Glorious Revolution. When he comes face-to-face with the end of his dream, an extraordinary scene takes place. As part of a group of Western doctors and intellectuals, he tries to cross the border from Laos into Cambodia. The group has a flag, a famous American actress, French intellectuals, and many doctors. At the border crossing, they attempt to make contact through a loudspeaker with the Cambodian soldiers on the other side. But no one answers. In that silence, he hears the truth: "Franz had the sudden feeling that the Grand March was coming to an end. Europe was surrounded by borders of silence, and the space where the Grand March was occurring was now no more than a small platform in the middle of the planet."

The silence that redraws this political geography is not the amorphous silence of the mass. The silence of the Khmer Rouge is murderous and total. It is the silence before the trigger is squeezed. The Silent Majority lives inside a padded cell in a state of permanent implosion. The silence of the Cambodians is *avant mortem*, the silence of the mass is *post mortem*. Between these two silences, the writer draws the panicked lines of his world. Baudelaire's albatross doesn't have the luxury of simply suffering derision anymore: he must, with his chained wings, ensure the survival of his tormentors. He is responsible for the world's new silences.

Private and public life are no longer distinct. Everyone must be several people under one umbrella, like Kundera's characters, in order to embody the necessary attempts to escape. Embodied in these characters are diverse but simultaneous dramas of the interior of one world unfolding inside another: there is the drama of love and sexuality, the drama of history with its relentlessly linear proceeding to which Kundera opposes the circular poetic of myth and of the "eternal return," and the tragedy of the poetic itself, which leads, within history, to a more and more "unbearable lightness of being."

All of which amounts to Fate. It is with Fate that Kundera scores his greatest novelistic victory. He restores the great conceit of the novelist as maker of worlds. He does not do this in old-fashioned innocence like the masters of the nineteenth-century novel, nor in willful ignorance like today's popular novelists. Nor does he put much store by the linguistic obsessions of writers in search of a subject. What he does instead is work right alongside his characters, shoulder to shoulder, as it were, helping them to the best of his and their ability to think out the clues of fate. He does not hide the fact that he is the maker of the clues. On the contrary, he illuminates them as much as he can, and since his characters are intelligent, they see them as well. But here is the amazing thing: no matter how well they see, or how much the novelist helps them, they will not heed them. They rush to their inevitable ends as innocently as all victims of sinister plots. Which is what they all are, intelligence notwithstanding: victims of inner compulsions, upbringing, power, ideology, kitsch, inattention. Their inner imperatives draw them, straight as a plumb line, to their ends. What is more, we recognize that they are us. This is because Kundera holds nothing back. He thinks and his characters think and the meditation is continuous, fluid, and finds immediate correspondence in our own process. Because he has not lost faith in the ability of the novel to perform at any depth, he does not hesitate to lecture on the writing of it, the structure of it, its paradoxical relation to reality. But none of it is boring, perhaps because he does not ask only the technical questions but also the questions that everyone asks. These questions are essentially philosophical, they have to do with the mystery of our being. To the magic realism of the South American novelists, Kundera brings something new, a kind of ontological realism, a magic essentialism. There is a generative power to Kundera's quality of attention to the present. The writing generates thought. Its fertility is far-reaching.

And yet, having committed himself to the paradox of living by questioning, Kundera has become the unwitting victim of his brilliance. Being unbearably famous precipitated a crisis. In order to stop being misconstrued, Kundera, who now lives in Paris, has stopped appearing in public or talking to journalists. The irony is very Kundera: having escaped from a society where he was not permitted to speak freely, he now lives in a place where he can't permit *himself* to speak freely. The difference between having silence imposed and choosing it is no doubt significant, but silence is silence. "As the mass media," the novelist tells us, "come to embrace and to infiltrate more and more of our life, kitsch becomes our everyday esthetic and moral code."

His tragicomic theme thus comes back to haunt him. The novelist, a Don Quixote born within literature, exploring horizons beyond it, an ontological investigator, comes face-to-face at every turn with himself in the process of setting out. He is operating at the center of what it means to be human in this age of "terminal paradoxes." Kundera's pantheon is inhabited by surprisingly few gods, many of whom are central European. There are Kafka, Hasek, Musil, Broch, Gombrowicz, in addition to Cervantes, Rabelais, Diderot, Sterne, Flaubert. Europe, or the idea of Europe, is another of Kundera's recurring themes. His insistence on the values of an idealized Europe, a sane, ironic, reasonable Europe, has irritated both the intellectual left and the new right. He has confronted Western Europe with an idea of Europe that was miraculously preserved in the oppressive darkness of a Soviet satellite. To the post-ideological left the existence of such clarity is an intellectual affront: Kundera uncovers a possibility overlooked by the leading lights of existentialism, structuralism, and post-Marxism, namely, the possibility that human beings can be helped to understand their situation through literature, and thereby save themselves. And surely, Kundera's lack of respect for traditional values, as evidenced by his passionate and lucid interest in the erotic, must be anathema to the right. This Central European placed at the center of current philosophical debates proves that the center is intellectually uninhabited though every human being alive today lives there. What does that say about thought in our time? That it, like an exile, is always where the action is not?

Paradox can be tremendously comfortable, and I am here to prove it. What is uncomfortable is the real situation of people in specific historical circumstances. Having been but a baby dissident myself, sent packing at nineteen for showing my milk teeth to the State, I never did experience the formative hells of a political prison in a workers' paradise. I have no doubt that given time (or the times, those wild mid-1960s), I would have been in an excellent position to do so. I had been headed that way, along with other writers of my generation, ever since the first thaw of 1963 when Khrushchev's de-Stalinization speech let some savage ghosts out of the bag of authorized history, including the unspeakable Gulag. All of a sudden, in those few heady moments before the Prague Spring, we could indulge in language like children in a swimming hole, not caring who watched or who got splashed. The beat of that *esprit du temps* saw young people from Bucharest to Detroit shed their planned futures to plunge headlong into the unknown. The generation gap, as it was known, transcended ideology. It was a revolt of the young against the old. The hair curtain suddenly became more important than the iron one. Solzhenitsyn's archival severity gave way to the avant-garde search for the mystery of self. The secret of Milan Kundera's art is hidden in that moment in the mid-1960s when the intoxication of freedom met headlong with the rediscovered tradition of European literature. What happened afterward is a story that renewed European literature and gave thoughtful people everywhere many new things to think about.

That brief mid-1960s abandon to the pleasures of ahistorical or even antihistorical self came to an end in Central Europe in the Prague Spring of 1968. From 1968 until 1979, paranoia and repression returned to the hung-over survivors of the sixties' romance with freedom. Like Kundera, and like myself, many writers and intellectuals chose exile to the West. But hardier souls had also been forged during the golden era of dissidence, people who refused to abandon the local fight for democracy and human values. They found themselves locked in a fight with the security apparatus, a body notoriously lacking in subtlety and humor. The tactics learned in the age of pranks and flowers gave way to sobriety and endurance.

In a shockingly brief time—testifying to a new millennial velocity—these people are now the new leaders of their countries. In November of 1989, an astonished Soviet woman told an interviewer for National Public Radio that she could not believe her eyes when she saw someone reading Solzhenitsyn on the Moscow subway. The same astonishing sights became commonplace in Prague when Kundera's books became widely available. And only one month later, Václav Havel, still in prison at the beginning of the year, became president of Czechoslovakia.

Václav Havel was cofounder (with Jiri Hajek) of Charter 77, the Czech human rights movement. Charter 77, founded in 1978, was formed to further democracy in Czechoslovakia, including monitoring the cases of citizens indicted and imprisoned for their political views. Its typewritten reports were widely circulated and carefully read. The human rights movement in Czechoslovakia, like its counterpart in the Soviet Union, was not intended for foreign consumption, though it got immense attention, particularly after the signing of the Helsinki Accords. The philosophical basis of Charter 77 was an amalgam of the best of 1960s ideals: nonviolence, openness, tolerance, democratic participation. These notions sound familiar today, as they issue from the mouths of the new reformers led by Gorbachev. For the new generation of leaders emerging today, the principles of Charter 77 are more urgent than ever, as they sketch the way to serious, not show, reform.

At the time of his arrest in January 1977, Václav Havel was a well-known playwright who had received worldwide attention for *The Garden Party, The Increased Difficulty of Concentration,* and *The Memorandum,* plays that raised fundamental human issues and questioned the place of human beings in a totalitarian society. While his plays make use of a large number of literary devices made familiar by the Theater of the Absurd, his political writings are straightforward. His 1975 letter to Dr. Gustav Husak, then president of Czechoslovakia, and his essay "The Power of the Powerless" are masterpieces of polemical writing. This combination of literary talent and moral integrity is peculiar to a number of Russian and Central European writers, part of a long tradition beginning with Tolstoy, but it is not as common as we have been led to believe here in the West, where dissidents have gotten big play this past decade. There are plenty of talents who'd rather switch than fight, and it's not entirely a dishonorable choice. Writers are, after all, writers, not politicians. It takes both a very special view of human beings in the world and a special world to produce that rare bird, the dissident writer.

On October 22 and 23, 1979, six signatories of Charter 77 were brought to trial in Prague. Havel received four and a half years in prison for disseminating unacceptable writings. He served most of his term but was abruptly released in January 1984 while he was ill with a raging fever. His *Letters to Olga* contain the majority of his prison letters to his wife. Some were censored and never delivered. The letters are numbered and dated, to give notice to prison censors that record-keeping is going on. They are also clear and unambiguous, which was a condition of censorship but is of great benefit to this writer who makes a point of clarity. Introspection is simple self-defense in prison, and Havel examines himself rigorously, chronicling and classifying his every mood. This activity soon gives way to reflections on what it means to be human in a century that has all but removed humans from the control of their destiny. Reflecting on the death of John Lennon, Havel has a generational epiphany. "I do not believe that certain values and ideals of the sixties have been discredited as empty illusions and mistakes; certain things can never be called into question, either by time or by history, because they are simply an indivisible dimension of the Being of humanity and therefore of history as well, though it is a history of repressions, murders, stupidities, wars and violence, it is at the same time a history of magnificent dreams, longings and ideals." While he stops short of religion, Havel nonetheless capitalizes "Being," seeing it as the focus of human activity, a "horizon" that imbues all our other "horizons" with meaning. The making of meaning is an active proposition, requiring faith, which is a mysterious and profound state. He now comes close to Milosz, but without Milosz's necessity of inventing a Supreme Evil, a Second Nature that demands absolute commitment. Havel sees no need for rejecting any philosophy or system of thought on the basis of its exclusivity. "Of eclecticism I have no fear whatsoever," he declares. "It seems to me foolish, impossible, and utterly pointless, for instance, to try to reconcile Darwin with Christ, or Marx with Heidegger, or Plato with Buddha. Each of them represents a certain level of Being and human experience and each bears witness to the world in his own particular way."

Born among the shards of postwar Europe under the totalitarian absence of thought imposed by rigid Marxist revision, the children of the 1960s availed themselves of all culture. Havel's eclecticism is not solely philosophical. It is cultural as well, and since censorship forbade him the specifics of Czech culture, we hear him discoursing seemingly at random on every book that falls into his hands, whether a Soviet history book or an old French novel. Attention to the particulars of each case, coupled with faith in Being (and thirst for it) amount to a kind of manual for survival in the world, not just in prison. Again, the generational rhythm is unmistakable: "a need to experience the world, again and again, in as direct and unmediated a way as possible." Prison memoirs have been philosophical since before Dostoevski, even when, as in the case of fantasist Jean Genet, it took Jean-Paul Sartre to "reason" out the philosophy. What distinguishes the thinking of this Czech dissident is his strong sense of generational solidarity which is exercised on the background of a powerful literary tradition. Kafka's name comes up quite often, and not accidentally. To Central European writers, Czechs in particular, Kafka was not a writer of allegories or parables. His writings are "truth," pure and simple. Kafka described for all times the enclosures of our bureaucratic nightmare. Kafka's vision is comforting to all disquieted souls because he confirms the enormity of the interior of our age. Havel finds in him the support that every Czech writer has found, including Milan Kundera, in a very different way. The differences are instructive. Havel is an excessively serious-minded writer, an impression that he is at some pains to disavow, describing himself at one point as a "merry companion," even inclined to mild "Don Juanism." This is a Havel we do not meet in these letters. We cannot imagine what Kundera's letters from prison would have been like, but one can assume a greater ease of manner, and a certain worldliness. At the same time, we can imagine Kundera trying to escape at all cost, never resigned or convinced of the necessity of paying for his freedom with confinement.

By his own confession, writing does not come easily to Havel. It may not come easily to Kundera ("From the sketch to the work one travels on one's knees"), but the appearances point otherwise. Havel is reverent, almost religious, while Kundera is a confirmed cynic. Havel is an activist who stayed in Czechoslovakia to fight even though first offered the choice of exile. Kundera has no great belief in heroism: his greatest lyrical weakness is nostalgia. Compared to Kundera, Havel seems almost sexless. One cannot imagine Kundera writing even a single communication without somehow referring to that essential mystery. Ultimately, these two Czech writers may represent two universal human types: the anxious self-investigator and activist and the robust but skeptical philosopher. Even though he is a playwright, Havel does not seem terribly interested in people (perhaps for fear of incriminating them). A kind of delicacy prevents him from observing humanity in ways other than universal. Paradoxically, Kundera, who is an avowed essayist, ends by poignantly communicating differences and thus creating unique characters. I have no doubt gone too far in comparing prison letters written under the shadow of censorship with novels composed in liberty. Nonetheless, there are two different kinds of mind at work here, sprung from a common time and land.

Václav Havel's letters deliver the reader to an important moment in the history of Central Europe. In what seems like only a few moments before *glasnost*, a voice is speaking clearly and intelligently about what is irreducible. Now that *glasnost* has become miraculous reality, we can see that President Havel's exploration of his own mind and soul has been both necessary and exemplary. It will provide a model for the emerging societies to explore and unsettle their collective conscience to levels deemed unimaginable only a few moments ago.

By the same token, Kundera's rejection of politics and seriousness will be the model for a very different social activity, a more anarchistic, younger, and less definable movement. Havel's moral decency is already being shadowed by a future inspired by Kundera's cynicism. Kundera asks, "When nature disappears from the planet tomorrow, who will notice?" Havel provides an uncertain answer through his suffering, which is a cry in the great silence now descending on us. Kundera asks, "What are the possibilities for man in the trap the world has become?" Havel, like Milosz, and like Kundera himself, with varying degrees of skepticism, puts his faith in imagination. Milosz is a maker of meaning on a white horse; Havel posits an abstract third "horizon" which imbues all other horizons with meaning; and Kundera, painfully amused, hacks away at the clearly hopeless windmills. No matter their positions, they have all been put outside by history, and they will avenge themselves by remaking the world. These "remakes" are only useful, however, in the narrow wedge of our particular time, moments before the East, like the West, awakens from its addiction to idealism. At that moment, all ideas, whether fabricated by genius or by television, by Karl Marx or by Karl Malden, will have no more currency than those of the nineteenth century. At that moment, imagination will become a commodity in the East as it is in the West, one among many, without any connection with reality. We live moments from the integration of the planet, but these are a dying man's moments: life passes before our eyes with a clarity never to be found again.

Death is the fertility god of the South American novel. It is also the driver of the magical countries invented by Latin Americans. Death is a familiar, one that does not particularly recognize many differences between itself and life. *La muerte* is human, almost a friend, compared to the technical coldness of Hitler death. Products of a schizophrenic history, divided between the fragmentary memory of an Indian past and a postcolonial world still in the process of definition, Latin Americans invent *approximate* countries. The circular workings of magical time continue visibly within the linearity of Western notions of progress. In Carlos Fuentes's *Terra Nostra*, modern Mexico meets hidden magic. The result is authentically familiar, truer than the official country. The things that go on in García Márquez's Macondo could issue their own daily gazette: they delight in the particulars of their existence.

After Don Quixote, heroes have been either too big or too small until they became, one sad day, the author. It was a moment every writer has rued without being able to get around it. It is fitting that a new notion of the hero should come from the same language that gave us the Don. The new magical-realist hero is someone who goes about doing the same kinds of things you and I do, the only difference being that the hero's doings have enormous consequences that reverberate. At least that's how Macunaima, the eponymous hero of Mario de Andrade's fantastic tale of Brazil, appears to operate. Macunaima is the distilled essence of Brazil, a magical being who embodies all the clashing cultures of that country, from Africa to the Amazon. Whatever he does is archetypal and bound to continue. When he spits, a swamp springs up. When he cries, flowers pop up. Different parts of his body create different things in the world. Just as easily, he can take certain things—coconuts, for instance—and replace parts of his body that have been mangled through stupidity or trickery. Macunaima's universe is generative and fertile like folklore itself, but like Marquez's Macondo, this is no folktale.

De Andrade was a prolific writer, innovator, and critic. By the time of his death, in 1945, he had succeeded in bringing Brazilian poetry into the twentieth century. The native surrealism of South America, influenced partly by French surrealism, came into its own in *Macunaima*, first published in 1928. This tale is the precursor of the entire Latin American school of magical realism, and is the granddaddy of books like Garcia Marquez's *One Hundred Years of Solitude*. *Macunaima* isn't just an ancestor, however. Like the hero himself, it is the original and the most fertile of the bunch. Macunaima, who can change his age, appearance, and race as he pleases, has lost a magical amulet. His search takes him to the great modern city of São Paulo, where his old magic meets the magic of machines. And herein lies a profound tale. The "car contraptions," "the photographic contraptions," and all the rest exercise a fascination for the hero that leads to much trouble. It takes him quite some time before he concludes that they have no soul. The encounters between the old sensual god and the new efficient god are painful. One *hears* the rending of the old fabric. Macunaima is fond of women and loses no opportunity to make love to them. Of his amorous wanderings universes are born, and new *living* phenomena enter the world. When he cannot make love, there is panic: the old world is running out of steam. In desperation he spies on lovers, and does his magical best to regain the amorous substance. (And the woman, if possible.) He is quite free of notions of morality, a concept belonging to the mechanical sphere. (Monotheism is already a primitive engine.) He will not work unless he is forced to by bad magic, and outside of making love he likes only to eat and sleep. These acts have consequences, though these may be—like morality—invented later to curb the exuberance of sheer being. Macunaima will never shy away from an opportunity to cheat anybody stupid enough, stupidity being the belief in the new order. Wisdom, on the other hand, is unapologetic living. Of course, he has no end of trouble because of it, and is often spurned, hexed, poxed, mangled, and even killed: he is operated on by the whole instrumentation of modern Brazil. Even streetcars are enlisted in the maiming of this god. But he also has terrible enemies in the cosmic realms where human technology is small potatoes: Vei, the Sun, will never lose an opportunity to lash his back with hot whips. The melancholy but undeniable existence of great undifferentiated energy makes this little god extremely human but also extremely important: without him there is no conduit between the spiritual and the material world. Without him the great energies operate directly within materials, which is the technological point precisely. The thin formal wall of human Imagination contains and redirects the cosmic energy. Macunaima is Imagination incarnate: he must be fertile so that Vei will not burn humanity to a crisp. But he also has friends, mostly small animals like birds and turtles, living things incapable of *ceding* a place to technology. The mystery of the placement of life within the smaller organisms is different from that of humans; it is a back road, a different way, and one increasingly important as roadblocks are set every few feet on the main (human) road.

Macunaima's story is a straight tale: this happened, then that. Compare its effortless unfolding with the neo-shamanism current today in most Western fiction. Of anthropological origin, neo-shamanism is mostly theoretical and it stays that way through "artistic" treatment. Poems, plays, sculptures, and "events" with shamanic themes (including Grotowski's theater) seem footnotes to scholarly books compared to tales like *Macunaima*. It is as if the new shamanism longs for an escape into literature, while

Macunaima, looking for his sacred amulet, is lovesick for a star. Once upon a time, Ci, who was once a woman but is now a star, made love to him in a hammock woven from her own hair. Macunaima is torn between immolating his hero self in Ci's great vortex and fighting for his uniqueness. In the end, Macunaima finds life on this earth quite worrisome and he joins his beloved Ci in the sky. He becomes the constellation of the Great Bear. It is *we* who now look at him with great nostalgia, wishing to annihilate ourselves in him. And here on earth, Mioritza wanders, telling his story. The touching pathos of this exotic but universally potent tale is about the infinitely sad meeting of two worlds, one doomed to die with the hero, another emerging brutally and unpoetically with the din of machines. The fertile world of myth takes our depth with it when it goes. De Andrade makes visible the withdrawal of the gods, leaving us flat and two-dimensional.

The fall into history is accompanied by mythic debris in Mario Vargas Llosa's *The War of the End of the World*. It is the end of the nineteenth century and a strange prophet has appeared in the backlands of Brazil. His name is Antonio the Counselor, and the wretched of the earth flock to him. He speaks of the imminent end of the world and of the Evil One, incarnated in the newly born Brazilian Republic and symbolized by taxes, civil marriage, and the separation of Church and State. The delirious community of the blessed that springs around the saint, repentant bandits, beggars, cripples, and starving peasants, finds itself in a strategically brilliant location at Canudos, where the prophecy says the City of God shall be located. As the City of God rises, with its two church towers, the political parties in the Brazilian capital at Salvador, one representing the old landowners, the other the rising republicans, focus their intrigues on the upcoming military intervention against the rebels.

But, wonder of wonders, the Bahian expeditionary

force sent by the governor is defeated. The next expedition, conducted by a real army, is savagely wiped out. Federal intervention is called for. An immense force, led by the Republican Robespierre of Brazil, heads for Canudos. The epic battle ends in the defeat of Brazil's crack troops at the hands of the believers. It is an unprecedented situation. The superstitious peasants ready to die at the drop of a sombrero for the glory of God stand for all the crazed masses of history, including those of our own times. There is something of the Ayatollah Khomeini, of Jim Jones, of the Eastern gurus in Antonio the Counselor. There is also the chilling intimation of the true mover of history, a force beyond reason and understanding. Galileo Gall, the anarchist, tries to understand by translating, as all ideologues do, into the pseudoscientific language of the left. Like the European intellectuals of the next century, he is ready to die for a cause he does not understand, or understands only in one dimension, that of a simple class logic. To him, the god-intoxicated masses of peasants are revolutionaries. In the natural exchange that has spontaneously appeared in Canudos as a result of extreme scarcity, he sees true communism. He is defeated by the irony of his misunderstandings: he dies not in battle but in the crux of a psychological bind for which there isn't yet any language. (Freud isn't born, psychology has not yet articulated itself among the ruins of myth.) Crudely drawn on the cave wall of history is the shadow of a future that has already begun killing.

Between the mythic authority of de Andrade and the historic grit of Vargas Llosa stretches the territory of García Márquez's magic realism, where Macondo occupies the heights. *One Hundred Years of Solitude* is the high Andes of imaginary (real) America. In Macondo history succeeds myth the way normal events (birth, marriage, death) succeed each other in human life. The regularity and normal logic of extraordinary events form the extraordinary substance of Macondo. One hundred years pass in orderly form (word follows word, sentence follows sentence, page follows page) before our eyes. We follow without protest the diminishing of miracles, the shrinking of the world, the withdrawal of the cosmos, the raising of the sky, the fall into a politics of asphyxiation. Macondo embodies our acquiescence to historical time—without losing the freshness of myth. It opens the possibility for the survival of imagination even as it illustrates its decline.

In *Chronicle of a Death Foretold*, a shorter tale, García Márquez treats the fall into history in spatial rather than temporal terms. He subjects the peasants of his Marquezian town to a metaphysical checkup. They line up at the author's door as if he were a visiting dentist. Each visit reveals the same thing: the infinite (in the form, often, of a fetching stupidity) lives inside every single one of them, connecting them with the ancestors and the gods. Shining through their cosmic stupidity is the light of fertility. But this isn't *illo tempore*: the State has constructed a bureaucratic structure (rudimentary, it is true), in case a Miracle should occur.

Which is just what happens. A bishop is coming to visit; at the same time, the villager Santiago Nasar is going to die. The two events are not connected but they are destined to connect. Everyone knows that Santiago is going to die: it is the most foretold death in village history. Santiago Nasar is killed. The bishop doesn't come, or rather passes by without touching. Everyone gives out a great sigh of relief. The outside world has been put off a little longer, myth's still stronger than bureaucracy. The new order is still only a seed (a large one, an incubus) inside the old one. When the bishop's boat almost touches the shore, the skin cracks a little. The light of historical time flashes briefly in, nearly blinding everyone. But the tale does not end with the narrow escape. Santiago Nasar resurrects. The tale starts again. García Márquez operates a prestidigitator's narrative circularity, a fictional hula hoop. His characters are made of the *slowest* mud while everything happens to them. They spin faster and faster, soon to be put into the orbit of history, but to themselves they appear to be standing still. The fall into history, when it comes, will be a great calamity, but only briefly. Then forgetfulness will set in. When Macunaima or the inhabitants of Macondo begin living in time, they lose more than the old stories. They lose the cosmos. They become metaphysically maimed creatures, amputated angels. The peasants of Canudos can win battles for God but are turned into dust by ideology. The moment of the fall is spectacular: the meteorite shower that covers the sky when angels fall is words. The writers stand beneath filling their inkwells. A rain of words falls for years over the spots where angels crash. Even bewildered travelers coming upon the crash sites accidentally begin speaking as if possessed. Mistaking the pretty fireworks for the total picture, they wallow in the ash, playing with the rapidly cooling fragments.

G. Cabrera Infante, a Cuban writer, is one who, though not unmindful of the origin of the catastrophe, stands in the word shower joyfully (painfully) shouting. His is the world after cinema, the city. Macunaima doesn't live here anymore, but the peasants of Macondo have come here after leaving their literal and metaphorical villages. The crowded favelas and tenements of the twentieth century are full of fallen angels. Cabrera Infante calls himself "the only English writer who writes in Spanish," and I take this to mean that translingualism is one step further into history, an entrance into the global village where everyone speaks English. His *Infante's Inferno* is an alliterative wonder, Joycean in the making of a city of language. He makes a bridge between Spanish and English, duplicating the bridge of movies and music that links his vanished Cuba with the world. He also makes visible the place where the wilderness of the old city gives way with an anguished twist to urban renewal.

Infante's parents were among the founders of the Cuban Communist Party in the 1930s: he must have grown up hearing architecture (the constructed future) in every sentence spoken late at night. Within this planned architecture, this cold verbal communism, the little boy grows hot, horny, awake, in a city that has outgrown planning and is now anarchistically reinventing itself. *Infante's Inferno* is a painstakingly elaborate reconstruction of the steamy sexual bath of pre-Castro Havana, a world now remote in time *and* space. Perversely and purposely apolitical, transtemporal and defiantly honest, the Proustian narrator of the book sweeps us irresistibly in his swell. Capable of entering every interstice of memory and unfolding every fold of its bygone geography, the adolescent teller lovingly recreates the city. Beginning *in utero,* this sexually precocious child of the tenements lives his life in pure expectation and constant pursuit of the sensual. He grows up surrounded by women, whose even chatter forms a nourishing music which is like the primal substance of language itself. (Somewhere in here must also be the purposefully excluded architecture of men's talk.) Infante encounters poetry, sex, and the city in the same breath. The rooms of the tenement at Zulueta 408 are the fabled doors of fairy-tale palaces, full of inexplicable mysteries, potential and real, like its maddening and often glimpsed partial nakedness, song, fights, and tropical dramas.

The bright daylight of Havana with its paralyzing heat finds its literal and metaphorical antithesis in the dark rooms of the cinemas where the American movies are. The stars of the 1940s inhabit the child and the adolescent with their impossible and magnified presence, molding his imagination and his dreams. The movies are already the future, as different from the reality of Havana as communist architecture, but whereas the movies speak to his eroticized being, architecture speaks to his (nonexistent) idealism. The ideology of consumption, cinema, is waging battle against his parents' ideology of class struggle. Reality is the battle's first victim. In the dark caves of the movie palaces imagination and sex claim the boy. He hunts for girls in the dark, with little success. He is, of course, hunting for the other, who could exist like himself within a circuit of rebellious desire. Likewise, Cuba hunts for an identity amid its imports and its racial contradictions, caught between colors, cultures, mythical debris, history, and posthistory.

Read on its simplest level, *Infante's Inferno*, like Dante's, is a journey of sexual initiation in which the circles of hell stand for the floors at Zulueta 408, or the neighborhoods of Havana. On another level, memory is its own circular hell, made all the more hellish by its seemingly endless repetitions of defeat compounded by uncertainty, getting smaller after each revolution. This inferno has its linguistic equivalent in an endless, obsessive, masturbatory punning in several languages. The political significance lies in what is omitted. Several times, the narrator begins to describe political violence, or aesthetics, or philosophy. Each time he stops himself, like a wise fool in a farce, and reminds himself and us that he is not to speak of those things. Those telling brakes are like the refrains of certain folktales: here is the rupture, here is what is missing, along this barely palpable seam the old worlds have collapsed. Desire serves him here as both a tool to jolt and make memory yield and a way to ride over these seams, these *barancas*, these *cenotes*. Sexuality is to Infante what anger is to Solzhenitsyn. Both are emotions in the service of memory, but also in the service of speed, the speed necessary to ride roughshod over the contradictory abysses where whole worlds have disappeared. The ending of *Infante's Inferno* is a crude joke. As in Kundera, it cannot be otherwise. Invention has been exhausted in the projection of such an exacting, world-committed memory (a word-movie): it has not found another imagination to join it, it has lost its demiurgic conceit, it has fully entered the West. After the erudite assault of cinematic puns, the world ends as a bad joke, the worst movie ever made.

Sky and earth are never very far in the fictive world of the Latin Americans. Even in Havana the sky *burns*. It is present in the skin, and in the siesta, and in the allure of coolness. Sky and earth have not yet separated as radically as they have for Westerners. Perhaps there is something in the language, still metaphorically and ontologically potent, that makes it possible to take anything and transform it; an angel miraculously uncombusted whose skin is equally resistant to abstraction.

P
A
R
T

F
O
U
R

Living
with
Amnesia

The map of exile resembles the radar maps used to track the movement of planes: shapes of light tracked across borders. It is all but invisible to anyone not paying close attention to it. Our fullest attention is given to other maps: the maps of multinational commerce and international tourism and terrorism, the maps of the mass media. Even literate and careful readers are largely incapable of reading the mythic map that underlies the constantly shifting map of current events. Much of the shifting comes from the mythic map, which sends shoots and wedges through the surfaces of the authorized world. The known world is only a small island in a sea of amnesia. Bolivian painter Suárez-Aráuz claims that "the world of amnesia and absences is a universe coexistent with the realm of memory and presences." The movement of exiles redraws the map to create areas of emergence for lost worlds. When one adds to this map the thousands of literary countries that have been with us since the beginning of imaginative writing, the challenge becomes retroactive. A question mark begins to run backward through history, putting all other cartography in doubt. It can be argued that all the imaginary countries of literature have been authored by literal or metaphorical exiles. Western consciousness is the creation of peripheral souls. Under pressure from them, the center must redefine itself.

The center of the West today lies in the electronic media, the first power in history capable of explaining itself continuously without losing strength, actually gaining through discourse. The infinite mechanical discourse has mechanized attraction to turn all our attention to itself. Its only challenge comes from the imaginings of outsiders who turn out, more and more, to include all human beings. The specific imaginings of real exiles are (however) still its most potent challenge.

Contemporary Western European and North American writers are not making an impression on this map for several reasons. The currency of imagination has been inflated by the demand in the West for the quick, painless scenarios of entertainment. Even the avant-garde does no more than produce "looks" for the market. Faced with the formal energy of an advertisement and a work of art, without knowing their immediate contexts, one would be hard put to decide which one is more "artistic."

Not having lost their "real" countries, Western writers seem stuck with alienation, which is a kind of psychological exile afflicting the entire society. Mirroring their splintering psyches, they end up producing models for the booksellers' seasonal market. The self-loathing produced by the inevitable sellout often gives birth to an antimaterialist idealism which, in turn, fuels the revolt against existing products and stimulates demand for new ones. The artist in the West is caught in a vicious cycle where the use of his imagination, no matter what his ideological sentiments, is the only thing required of him. The mechanical center is indifferent to the moral qualms of its fuelers. It needs words to keep the discourse continuous and self-canceling, bereft of gaps and silences which alone can make it grind to a halt. Gaps and silences can have the effect of creating emphasis, which is what the center is set up to prevent. All words must be equal; there should be no stresses; self-referentiality must reign. The machine is egalitarian: emphasis can reintroduce recently marginalized humans into the center. They will not be allowed to crawl back in through gaps in artistic production.

The situation of the exiled writer is quite different. His entire existence is predicated on a gap. The basic, material facts of breaking with one's entire sensorial universe put a different kind of strain on the imagination, which is called to replace the lost world with another. If it fails, the artist goes under his weight of nostalgia and impotence into that well-mulched swamp of heartbreak and failure that is our century's chief product. An exile must not fail, but "not fail" at what? Making an alternate reality, a different world, one that can resemble only superficially the lost ones, is an enterprise of fundamental failure, even if by some unrelated process it does become a public success. The only thing an exile cannot fail in is his *faith*. The faith in the made thing is what is so distressing and so important. And why the creations of exiles have gained a central part in contemporary discourse, and why they mean trouble for the central machine. For all their imaginative skills, Western artists have specialized in loss of faith. The innumerable artistic crises of our century have revolved about a continual loss of faith in everything but in art above all. The irony is that art is becoming both the new currency of our time and the single most potent product of our information society. A funny time to lose faith! On the other hand, it is precisely the faithless quality of the contemporary art product that gives art its value. Into this inflated currency, the exile now brings an absolute standard of value guaranteed by a fanatical faith. What is the response of the market? Panic.

Western artists are not taking kindly to this invasion by exiles. As peripheral people in charge of shoveling art into the maw of the center, they demand of these exiles who are (clearly!) the peripherals of the periphery to make sense of their freedom. The cultural slum raises defenses against the culturally homeless because it is asked to provide a creative space that it does not possess and has no idea how to take back from the electronic media. The exiles do know how, and know how through their exile, which is a fundamental loss of all centers, private and public. Exiles thus find themselves in the odd position of attempting to take back the center of the West, an operation Westerners themselves cannot perform.

Marcel Corniş-Pop finds an "interesting parallel (to the situation of the exile) in a certain trend in American literature that emphasized the 'inner exile' of the disinitiated, outcast, floating innocent, dangling man." But the dangling men of Bellow, Updike, et al. are not exiles. They are only appendages of the machine that has ground them, sad flags of defeated flesh flying from camera dollies. Theirs is not exile but disintegration. There is no room for the "dangling man": he dies of suffocation.

Commenting on Corniş-Pop's remarks, Christopher Carduff asks: "Have you noticed, too, that since the late sixties many American novelists have dropped the 'dangling man' figure for the more powerful figure of the 'literal exile' when exploring the angst of the times? Bellow's dangling man, Updike's rabbit (circa 1959), Percy's movie-goer, Heller's Slocum, have given way to Bellow's Mr. Sammler (a Polish Holocaust survivor living in New York), Updike's Col. Elleou (in *The Coup*, the exiled ruler of a mythical African land called Kush), Roth's Amy Belette/Anne Frank in *The Ghost Writer*, and Styron's Sophie in *Sophie's Choice*. This suggests not only the place the exile holds in the Western public's collective imagination, but also the need of even the most *native* imaginations in America to appropriate the exile and his themes to lend moral weight to their novels."

In literal exile there is a kind of health: the exile moves outside and his ambition is to create something as spacious but qualitatively better than that provided by the present geopolitical boundaries. Faced by the inhuman electronic center, all artists feel bound to make unquantifiable "things" out of language. Yet Western "unquantifiables" become rapidly quantifiable and are sold practically before they are made. Western postmodernist language makes itself autonomous out of shards. The sound of the West is the noisy silence of the mass bombarded by "live talk," which is not really live but electronic. The native periphery builds alternatives from the detritus of culture.

Exiles have not yet despaired of culture. The immediate effect of their faith in art is the kind of pleasure of the text that liberates rather than asphyxiates. In Western art, bodies are not disposed of as in real life, in blood-curdling innocence one by one or by the thousands, but rather in blood-curdling calculation, and in slow motion, for the increasing numbness of the spectator mass. Instead of disposing of a *whole* individual, everyone is killed *a little*. Instead of a few dead, we are looking at vast masses that are all *a little dead*, though they still ambulate. Painless, generalized, democratic death sprouts from the invisible psychic wars. The imaginative literature of exiles commands a still-active network of structures within which each death is a grand event.

The mechanical center (from here on, called simply the Center) takes in the products of culture and returns them de-contented, unmeaninged, empty. A poem passing through television or a painting through Sotheby's gives up the ghost of its meaning and is returned to the world as meaningless commodity, defanged and blank. Both TV and Sotheby's use the extracted juice to keep running: they are fueled by the meaning they consume.

The Center is the engine of the Empire, the motor of Power. It is important to capitalize this triumvirate because it represents the main antihuman force operating in the world today. The media Center empowers the status quo of the new World Empire (McLuhan's Global Village) to marginalize human beings until they are no more than producers of fuel for the new god Techné.

The authority of the Empire rests on its ability to represent creation (and human life) as meaningless. This is possible as long as the products returned by the Center are read uncritically, that is, are seen as defanged and denatured. To read critically is to read with power. Every exercise of individual power drains the Center. The Center produces a single, monotonous discourse in which all elements are equal. While this discourse is intended to have the same effect—concentrating power and debilitating humans—its construction is different in East and West.

I'm using "East" here to stand for word-based Communist and Third World bureaucracies, and "West" for high-tech nations. My East is a specifically European term that includes Central Europe, and refers to a world made in the Stalinist Fifties and the Revisionist Sixties from the tattered remains of Marxist-Leninism and Groucho Marxist–John Lennonism. The East remains, for me, the totalitarian place where I grew up slanted, the place that defines the terms of my adolescent rebellion, and that of the 1960s. Psychologically, every system of restraint-artistically-resisted is the East. The recent revolutions in Central and Eastern Europe have not eliminated the East of which I speak, which is permanently set in the soul of my generation now coming into power. That East is the mirror in which the West is reflected. Neither the historical nor the psychological fact of this East has changed. What *has* changed is the access of the West to this East, the removal of the Wall keeping out the river of commodities. Likewise, the East, in all its imponderable senses, will now flow into the West. A new creature will be born from the joining of the Berlin Wall with the Berlin Mall.

Until World War I both East and West used words to compose the discourse of power. Before that time the main job of empires had been the deforestation of the world, followed by the maintenance of the letter of the texts made from the murdered forests. The Victorians, for instance, killed all the English oak and the Americas' mahogany to give birth to their libraries. The books and furniture among which the imperial brains grew large came to a sudden end in World War I. Since then, the West has switched to an image-based discourse, while the East still lumbers on along the linear paths of print.

The collapse of empires after World War I was also a collapse of their central discourse, a breakdown that has released a swarm of genius that is still active. Kafka's provincial German, issuing from the periphery of Austro-Hungary, has an authority no centrally sanctioned discourse has yet managed to recoup. It comes, like Freud's, from the shadow of large Biedermeier cabinets, the last of their kind to remember the forest. The collapse of central imperial discourse was also the end of classical literatures. In that vacuum we heard the sudden voice of the peripheries. The so-called "minor" literatures became the expressive home of human beings. As the empires of the West were reconstituted post–World War I along image-based discursive lines, their only challenge came from the word-charged periphery. Every peripheral country in the world contained an active creative element busy recreating or creating its identity even as it was vanishing. As these countries' word-based bureaucracies consolidated their grip on power, they expelled these dangerous writers—formed by the gas clouds of the blasts of World War I—into the West. There they found new homes from which to continue the challenge. The powers of the West switched hastily to the electronic brain, whose projective power is still the exclusive property of its centers. On the face of it, it might seem absurd that something as vast as the industrialized world would switch from word to image because of a challenge from the flotsam of a defeated world. But technology is challenged by whatever impedes its development toward autonomy, and nothing impedes it better than a human with a cosmic chip on his defiantly raised shoulder. This uppity critter does not depend solely on words for his increasingly untenable claims to centrality but has an infinitely more difficult time doing so in images. Nonetheless, the faith expressed here is that the demiurgic force does not have to confine itself to a single technology (writing/print). We are now inside a circuitry that does not have human interests at heart, and which has expanded its discourse of both words and images to cover nearly the whole planet.

The East has operated chiefly by means of words regulated by the official syntax of official ideology. The relation of this word machine to community defined until recently the moral stance of the Central European and Soviet writer. If you went with the flow, you garnered its rewards. If you didn't, you disappeared. Simple. The luxury of being a tolerated outsider was not available, which may have been a good thing, since a tolerated outsider is only a slumming insider. Societal institutions were ruled by the same syntax. The family, which Marx originally saw as an extension of private property, was restored under Stalin, and became "the basis of society." Community formed outside family and State became impossible.

The State operates by obscuring itself to its inmates. They are not allowed to *see* the working of the communal machine. They are only allowed to *hear* the clattering of its rhetoric. Lenin's formula: "Socialism = The Power of the Soviets + Electricity" implied a possible illumination. In the West the State knows how to prosper under the glare of publicity. In the East, the darkness of the prerevolutionary print shop still reigns. For decades, the only community that people were allowed to hear was the din made by the house of words the State built. They were allowed to hear the emptying of their language, the sound of the word-sea sucked through the huge teeth of Soviet dams, which made not electricity but obscurity. The word-sea, a continuous tape that was part of everything, and which constituted official reality, made a B-flat sound, the same B-flat that the post–big-bang universe makes, as well as machinery (including pipes in the walls). The people were compelled to hear themselves as words, as parts of speech. The long speech of State communism held everyone behind the bars of its syntax. It was a monotonous, vast, comforting speech. In the sea of Castro's seven- hour speeches, the masses were waves. The Politburo spoke and spoke. Writers were to be watched within this sea like weather fronts. In their ability to change word order, hence upset community, they were all potential squalls, typhoons, hurricanes. The Kremlin was the fountainhead of the megaflow of language, the little house of speech that pumps out the seas. The technicians in the pumping station attended to their dials, carefully controlling the direction in which the language flowed, and the possible threats to it. Under the sea of words, placed strategically, were little prisonhouses of language full of dissidents, especially bewildered Marxists. But, of course, the whole sea was a prisonhouse, each word serving the function of obscuring vision, of cutting off the view, of dismissing the outside.

In the 1960s the politically loosened syntax unleashed a new tribe of writers. They turned some words inside out. It was fun: they had at their disposal the huge rhetorical word-machine of the State. They played games with censorship, which was the grammar of their community. Its rules governed proper speech. Literature was the vernacular, bound to break the rules, but until then it was a mutually comforting relationship with well-defined borders. In the 1960s, quite suddenly, censorship became the agent of an entire literature outside its edicts, a literature of exclusion. The excluded language found itself paradoxically helped into the outside by censorship, the guardian of the interior. This community outside the official community, the uncensored wilderness of samizdat, this breeding ground for exiles, may be the twentieth century's most native phenomenon.

My books came into being as products of my banishment. The censor has, in a sense, also fathered them. Under normal circumstances, most creations, whether human or literary, have only a mother and a father. Under normal circumstances, the mating of language with an author brings forth a book. In the perverse lands of ideology, there is a third parent, the censor. Human beings have to share their beds with the State. This tripartite origin pertains to all Eastern Europeans, and to their products. The tension between conventional Oedipal interiority and the activities of the Ministry of the Interior give birth to the monsters of exile.

At the crossroads of bureaucratic communism and the involuntary nomads it has produced stands Kafka. Without him everything would be incomprehensible. This provincial Jewish clerk writing in provincial German in a provincial town wrenched from a once great provincial empire has the fullest set of marginal credentials an artist could ever hope for. There are fewer minds better positioned for obscurity. At the same time, he stands at the precise juncture of East and West, word and image, old interior and new interior. He is Janus the scribe.

The position of Kafka between interiors is explosive: he bends to drink from the secret spigot of the future, already installed into the corpse of the nineteenth century. The hallways of the immense bureaucracy where he works link past and present. The past has ornamental and infinite clerk factories that give directly into the twentieth century's new interiors of camps, prisons, holding cells, gas chambers, control towers, listening posts. The past and future clerks clerking in these chambers are engaged solely in the production of new interiors. Their speciae always *sub aeternitatae* has forgotten how to live outside. They are the silent majorities silently huddled about internal internecine interiority, from Party rank and filers to the narcoleptic TV masses of the West. There is very little room between Kafka's growing bugs and the walls they continually produce to hide themselves in.

Dissident literature everywhere has been activated by

Kafka. A tall building can be made from all the passages written by dissidents on the architectures of their bureaucracies. Police halls mirrored into infinity traverse their writings: the dissidents themselves use these to travel from one text to another. The maps of camps, the blueprints of ministries, the scrawls on cell walls, the assembly lines, the holes of gas chambers: the blueprint of the twentieth century. All these numbered numberless interiors are a single place, a growing labyrinth at the center of which sits monster minotaur Kafka scribbling the escape routes. He can't be removed by the Center because he is a god, the Daedalus behind the whole labyrinth, the mapmaker. He sits there with his prophetic bug hatchery made from mirrors, a god who embarrasses his creation but is still powerful because he is a fouler of distances, a relativizer of metric certainties. He makes the far near and the near far but always connected to himself, to his vision. Literature activated by his *trompe l'oeil* Fata Morganas is a destabilizer.

On the other hand, Kafka, a tourist, may have simply walked the wrong way, away from the tourist attractions prepared for the group, and been the first to arrive in the new interior, a time traveler who slowly became cognizant of the true size of the place, of its infinity, its generative speed, and its true shape. He makes it impossible for anyone *not to know*. Dissident literature sets up Kafka's mirrors at the intersections of private and public life. Reflected there are bureaucrats, myriads of them, stripped of their functions, detached from power, hideously human. Hysteria ensues, hysterical laughter, fear, irruptions of religiosity, renewed institutional terror. It is a terrible vision and it cannot be forgotten. Dissident literature opens a crack in the censor, making his job immensely difficult; in addition to censoring he must now ensure that the wide crack of self-consciousness will not break up the huddled bugs.

The problem of seriousness is much greater for the

Communist bureaucrat, who has taken self-important adulthood for his model, than for the capitalist consumer, whose model is adolescence. The danger to the adolescent is not hysterical laughter caused by a sudden, unbearable paradox, but an irruption of self-consciousness followed by the revelation of emptiness.

The censor's job is to make sure the authorized text is produced without cracks and irruptions. They must combat the Kafka devices cropping up everywhere, but how to do that when the devices mirror precisely the interiors of the authorized text? It is a subtle nightmare that will eventually leave only one solution to the beleaguered Communist: switch from word-base to image-base, that is, become capitalist.

Against the authorized text, exiles have invented a number of devices. One of these is the imaginative memory that thrives on excess. To remember unabashedly, monstrously, sensually is to test the convenient versions of the past. Remembering like this quickly exhausts the officially allotted quotas of nostalgia. This is ontological remembering, *anamnesis*, the flashback that contains everything in brilliant detail. Memory in exile is powerful, it has hair triggers that can go off on the most tenuous analogies. Slow architectural writers, like Solzhenitsyn, reconstruct with painstakingly realistic precision, but the release of various narrative or lyrical contents out of the cages of the past is an avalanche. A calculated anger is the catalyst for this kind of remembering, mixed with a sense of cosmic justice. The compressed anger spills into epic lamentation.

Czeslaw Milosz's memory is made of another, quicker substance. Its chemistry, like Proust's madeleine, is only partly reconstructive (architectural), because it rises in a single wave. Milosz's words point outward even as they record a lost interior. This "out" is a past experienced mythically now, its active memory is a force like the imagination, working not to entrap things but to release them. It sends for them, like the immigrant who brings his family out years later. Once they arrive they are enlisted in a moral crusade, alas; but nobody can deny their existence.

Milan Kundera, on the other hand, has no memory at all. He fills in the spaces where the feelings are with details that seem appropriate but are in fact wholly imaginary. It is by this method that I have written my autobiography. My past was dotted with faceless feelings to which I affixed facts. They were powerful enough to evoke the admiration of my mother, who before the book came out remembered things quite differently. The power of the printed word— already an authorized text—had falsified my mother's no doubt truer memories. One of the first jobs of authorized text is the switching of memory cassettes: it replaces your own with an official one.

The imaginative memory of exiles, no matter how imaginary, still holds on to its faith in content, making pure self-referentiality impossible. It is this, more than anything else, that challenges the Center. In the West writers are pretty much imprisoned in self-referentiality. Those whom the gods wish to destroy they first make self-referential. To the extent that exiles feel themselves to be the agency of a mystery that uses them, an opening remains, both for escape and habitation. In culturally or politically authorized writing, the author works to bring words into the fold. Official grammar is both the ram's horn that calls them home and the corral where they are housed. But the excessive rememberer scatters the words, turns the signs around. The faster he does this, the harder it is for Center Control. Speed and fury are the creative necessities of our time for responding adequately to the speed and force of technological interiorization, including the ever-growing self-referentiality of contemporary writing.

Western Marxists today criticize literature for its claims to autonomy. They cannot allow for the existence of language outside ideology. The notion of the outside is suspect to them, as it should indeed be to all ideologues or proponents of a central discourse of any kind, whether it be "scientific" or "humanistic." The Outside, which is to say the Unknown, was abolished, in the Marxist view, by late capitalism in the nineteenth century. The expansion of markets in that century eliminated the unknown, which had been only the exotic all along. They would have us believe that Arthur Rimbaud was the last poet with a legitimate claim to the Outside because his was the last escape into the last unknown possible while still maintaining authorship. Clearly, the Outside is here seen mostly in its geographical dimension, but geography is destiny for any materialist worth his salt. Rimbaud's defection to Africa and "escape" into commerce marked the end of the individual hero, the end of escapes. With Rimbaud, poetry and imagination were forced to abandon their claim to other realities because all realities had been colonized by trade. Rimbaud, the person, realizing this great Marxist truth, abandoned poetry and took up commerce. From this sensible action to the next sensible action, which is to write propaganda for the State, is only a short step. A sensible person realizes when the jig's up.

Alas, for Marxists, poetry and imagination can go farther than the person traveling with them. Even if Rimbaud stopped, his poetry did not, nor did his successors, who continued to assault the Unknown as if Marx had never been born. True, one has to go farther and deeper into exile in order to escape the market and Marx. One has to question radically the person carrying the virus of dissent to make sure that a small portion remains inviolate from M and M.

This portion, called the soul, is also the source of the faith that activates resistance today. Marxists go to great lengths to maintain the person while maintaining that the person is nothing more than an assemblage of impersonal forces. This apparent paradox allows for such things as the cult of personality: if the person is only an anthology of forces, then may the best anthology be exalted! Rimbaud, however, *abolished himself* before he could be so easily "read." He envisioned the coming of the "red cities," the advent of the collective Rimbaud, the mass acting like an intoxicated individual. And he wanted none of it. It is not capitalism that abolished the unknown of the individual but Rimbaud the individual who abolished capitalism, and all economic theory with it, including Marxism. Rimbaud was not an "author" (the holder of a copyright) but a force: he released the world instead of arresting it. He was an anti-author who abolished not only his "I" ("I is another") but also his posterity. The Marxists can rail on about "markets," but they know nothing of the imagination. Imagination is demiurgic. It creates the markets it saturates, overthrows, and transforms. The Marxists profess no gods, therefore they cannot imagine *a place* for the imagination outside of its concretions. They ask, "Where is it?" as they do of God. Everything has to be "somewhere": it has to be situated within the system; it must be part of the dialectical machine. They are without ontological memory because a "beginning" implies a creation *ex nihilo:* they do not remember either their conception or their origin. They have no world prior to ideology. They reproduce within the text of their own interpretations. They have even exchanged history for a reading of it. This is why the only Marxists to be found today are in universities. The determinism of the classroom is the only place where they can operate. Not only are they producers of theoretical interiors (better mousetraps) but they cannot function outside of them. (There is a long waiting list for new units before they are even built!) The worker, that ideal history-making Marxist, has been eliminated by Marxist criticism. The worker has become a sign, a prefix attached to certain bordering nouns in order to cement them.

In the Soviet Union the State was the sole reader of reality, and thus the only Marxist. The Marxist thinkers themselves became parts of the speech of the State, bordering prefixes. They kept in the restless populace. The rigorous grammar of the State had only one enemy: non-Party writers. These writers were counter-nouns, agents of cement-crumbling time, or perhaps something more insidious, a whole linguistic wrecking crew.

Roland Barthes and the French school expanded the words *writing* and *reading* to take in everything. The world, they said, is a text, therefore it can be read. Previously "dense" areas become intelligible: signs connect in a language. The world becomes flat like the page. It is, of course, a text without a single "author." There are "authorized" portions of it, which constitute the easily readable part, the part that also serves the interests of power. The authorized texts are, in fact, the specific contracts between their authors and the structures of power. Authorial intention "writes out" what the power structure wants forgotten. What it "writes in," the final readable version, is only a record by default of what it has suppressed. The library is the repository of the official text. The rest of the text, the hard-to-read part, has not really disappeared. It has merely been relegated to an Outside. This Outside is vast, expansive, changeable, paradoxical, perverse, traversed by all the escape routes. It is filled with tension, movement, instability, and force. Its pressure causes authors and authorized texts to shift, to sink, to crack, and to explode. What has been repressed returns through these cracks and destroys the order of the status quo. The erased Outside text sometimes reappears quietly, like an erased file on a computer disk, but often it surges cataclysmically, the way the new fundamentalist readings of the Koran and the Bible are doing today. Hermeneutic wars have their own timetable. The exilic text is likewise liable to irrupt within approved literature.

The countertext, whether it is a new reading or a new writing, is a gate that shuts behind its (non)authors. The outside of exile where (non)authors find themselves is hell before it is heaven. Exiles write in a language they are quickly losing, their references gone. As their world shrinks their poetry burns. When they abandon their old language for a new one, most of them are lost. This is true for many Romanians of my postwar generation. One would assume that the survivors—those who made a successful transition—are now true liberators. Alas, this isn't the case because neither the interior nor the Outside has fixed boundaries, and their struggle continues even as they define each other.

The successful countertext often returns, to take its place in the canon from which it was expelled, like Solzhenitsyn or Kundera's books in the era of *glasnost*. Sometimes exiles themselves return, like Lenin. In any case, the world that has once expelled them will not be the same afterward. The record of power is rewritten under the pressure of their authority until it will become *nothing but the story of returnees*. Slowly, their heroic struggle to break through the approved text will become the approved text. As in fairy tales, the hero returns to become the new king. The returnee is the model hero through whose actions power circulates to stay fresh. Returnees are celebrated because they have seen the Outside and have brought back information about it, making it ready for conquest. Their descriptions (travelogues, memoirs, journeys through hell) are blueprints of colonization. Their countertext-become-record will now help the interior to grow by annexing the Outside as reported by these former exiles. The story is exemplary: once upon a time dissidents came up against the machinery of power and were forced Outside (thus having all their interiors violated: familial, civic, professional), and then after great trials they returned with the Outside inside themselves, having proved themselves greater than the world. Everything they encountered Out There was grist for the mill which eternally grinds the desire to return. Crusoe comes back from his island with perfect confidence in his ability to recreate civilization while elaborating, simultaneously, his fantasy of return.

But returnees do not really bring back the Outside (which remains gloriously potential), but only representations, images, ideas, hallucinations, that is, a *text*. It is only one text among many, but it is this text, the collected-hallucinated-interpreted Outside, that will become the new canon and no doubt a new basis for exiling those who would challenge it. The new text of power will replace the old power record and gain enough strength in the process to conquer the (imaginary) places newly described. Into them Power sends containers of all kinds—plows, roofs, domes, and surveying instruments—to measure, divide, and settle the hallucination. Countries appear, and barbed wire. The returnee has now become the author of an imaginary portion of the Outside which he has made into a new interior. He has built a recordable "I" out of renouncing his exile. What began as banishment ends as a desire to consume. The authorized record expands, the Empire grows.

In the diminished Outside (no less diminished for being diminished in an imaginary dimension), the pressure increases proportionally to the sophistication of the Empire's recuperative power. Unable to colonize something that, after all, remains generically potential, the Empire perfects ways in which to deny the existence of any Outside not on the record: it does not exist, it is not shown on TV, it is structurally (scientifically) impossible, it is akin to the belief in angels, it is *absurd*. The only Outside possible is the one described by the most recent returnees.

Seldom, however, do exiles return. Their escape has made them permanently a part of the countertext. They produce the unapproved literature that exists eternally parallel to the records of power. This countertext records fabulistically, aphoristically, paradoxically, obliquely, the existence of an outsider tribe that is home only when away from it. Voluntary exiles and bohemians are part of this tribe. They are not coming back on purpose; they make good their escape. They do not read their new surroundings into the record. They defend themselves with imagination-produced counter-tools, anti-interiors, unpredictable movements, nomadic mysteries. Above all, they usurp the author. For all that, it is increasingly difficult to live Outside in the contemporary world. The desert once available to the saints is a testing ground for nuclear weapons. Assuming a different identity in the age of computers is no easy task. Being heard only by those one intends to be heard by is impossible in the giant Ear the world has become. The solution is to make the countertext so resemble the text that the defenses are fooled. The tonal ambiguities developed by oppressed cultures to communicate different things in the same words to friends and foes become urgently important.

It would seem that reading the world's text is an activity that allows mystery only one virtue, that of being explicated. The whole world becomes a Borgesian library. Sections of this library are authorized, others are not. The unauthorized texts (the erased, successful escapes) stand shoulder by ghostly shoulder next to those we are made to see. (This is true in the East and in the West, though in different ways.) The spiral staircases that connect one section to another are a complex nervous system whose intricacies an explorer (reader) can travel forever. This vision is not one of unredeemed interiority, because the signs that can be read aren't just *there*. They also can be *invented*. Imagination can change, erase, or increase the text in any direction it pleases. Whether pressuring the official record or giving "flatness" other dimensions, it is the demiurgic force, par excellence. It is trans-authorial: it uses the brain that uses the hand. It is everywhere creation occurs, and creation occurs everywhere. Most important, it exists in opposition to what it creates. Its creations are its enemies. In order to overcome them, and prevent itself from being extinguished, it must create even more. Imagination is increased by the necessity to overcome its productions. The virtual and the created are at war. Imagination is not the imagination *of* anything: it is a pure force, an expressive illumination, a demiurgic irruption that creates the world in its swell. Contents and their respective forms crystallize in its wake, making it necessary for it to continue irrupting in order to destroy these formations. In its crystallized form imagination operates in the authorized world. In its irruptive mode it resides Outside. It is "natural," then, that institutional interiority must first attack the free play of imagination.

The integrity of imaginative movement is suffering mega-assaults at the moment. In the West, the fake imagination of the entertainment industry is seeking to replace the organic, primary, connected, active imagination of human beings. The institutionalization of the imagination is one of the main concerns (if not *the* main concern) of both major political interiorities. In the East, the crude hand of the State has entered the process directly. In the West, the State replaces the free play of the mind with programming. The two modes, brutality and narcolepsy, respectively, have different effects.

To guard from its own detritus and to survive, the role of the imagination in a commodity-driven culture is to strip bare the images. To imagine *nothing*, or rather *the* nothing behind all the layers of simulacra and false nature, becomes its primary mission. Imagination, in our image-clogged *fin de siècle*, must become an image destroyer, a torcher of imitations: not a maker of images but a maker of truth, a philosopher. It must retain the imaginative (and destructive) qualities of fire (the world's first TV), but without the exploitative contents of mass-culture projections. Fire is generative while TV (the cold fire) frames every projection. Imagination cannot be utopian: utopia is now the business of mass production, Disneyland. Anti-utopian, anti-artistic, anti-imaginary, imagination in the West today must meet monastic exigencies and display, above all, a great *sobriety*. Imagination has become the custodian of the real, and because of this it must defend itself from illusion, a job made immensely difficult by the complete hold of illusion on everything, especially desire.

All images want to become one image, the Sacred Image, the Icon. The tractor-mounted-fur-wrapped pudgy Russian boss is pasted over the Byzantine Christ. The new Coke (the Romantic) covers the old Coke (the Classic). The icons of the East battle with the desire of the mass to worship the icons of the West: the pudgy boss is dying for a Coke (the Holy Virgin next to the head of Lenin over the shipyard gate at Gdansk). In the West icons are under fire from one another: numberless pretenders lie buried under the Golden Arches. Icons, East and West, ask only for worship. It is the only way we can speak to them because they do not speak our language. Our only contact is the altar where we deposit our energy in them. Before television, the powerful icons that surround us used to be kept in check by a critical discourse aided by art: words born of contradictions revealed by collage. But collage has only enriched the icons. To imagine nothing does not mean to revert to the ideological authorization of the word once more, or to some other symbolic order. We simply don't know what that nothing is: we have not yet imagined it. The icons that orbit around us multiply quickly: they are a space prison. Unlike words, images do not overthrow each other: they join up. To get beyond them we need to know how to disrupt their joining. We become flatter as they become more multidimensional: each trick of perspective that we dispose of, they take up. Eventually we may become mere images, trapped like shadows in some collective hell, the United Fascist States of Utopia. In another generation, people raised by images will not be able to imagine escape. The walls of Plato's prison-cave will be animated.

In
the Eye
of the
Ghost

In 1965, Italy was the answer to my prayers. From the moment I landed in Rome under an impossibly blue Mediterranean sky, I was awash in color. The monochromatic political posters on Romania's peeling walls from which the triple folds of Communist leaders' chins hovered over the populace faded as I abandoned myself into the azure arms of women holding particolored chocolates. Advertisements were like childhood, while the posters of our leaders were dour adulthood and grim reality. Here were books. At the outdoor market near the train station in Rome I found a Bible in Romanian. The Bible was on bible paper, well bound. I looked carefully around when I bought it: there was no whispering, no applause, no cries of anguish or delight. I could not believe that the humans around me could go about so blithely unaware of the momentous exchange. Incredibly, however, it was just that: cash for the Bible. I opened it immediately to the Revelation of John and I stood there, under the Roman sky, experiencing the euphoria of the end. The tension of years of book terror and delights of imaginary libraries left my body like a soul. I was not yet aware of its departure but something went slack in me and a hole opened.

I began to devour books, sleep books, dream books. But these books, suddenly so easily available, were not the same in a world where reading was not secret. And the things I had to say seemed to have lost something when said out loud. They had carried more weight whispered, and certainly more power forbidden.

Italy was still part of that bookish Europe whose son I was. It was not until I got to America in 1966 that I began to rethink the place of the book in the scheme of things. America was, above all, loud. My generation, twisted about by a fierce and illuminated *esprit du temps*, was experiencing things that no books had yet been written about. This may well be true of every generation but mine was particularly visionary and internal, and the speed with which we made our discoveries made it impossible to create anything but a poetic record. Reportage was dead for all practical purposes: there just wasn't enough time.

I struggled with the volume of my voice. It took me at least two years before I could speak in a normal tone about politics or art or drug-visionary experience. I lowered my voice automatically on these subjects, maintaining all the while the elegant obscurity of phrasing that had been the necessary cover where I came from. I spoke with quiet passion of urgent matters in a manner that must have seemed at best esoteric to the fellow Americans of my generation, who liked to turn up the volume on their stereos. And yet I was much closer to them than to the brahmins of the American literary mainstream, who seemed to me no better than the literary bureaucrats of Romania, though concerned with careers rather than ideology. The fast-moving Americans of my generation, to whom my bookish, Eastern European discourse was addressed, were TV children. For them, books were objects to be neither venerated nor attacked: they were just there, like everything else in the society of consumption and spectacle—things to be consumed, to be amused by, or to get some practical instruction from.

I was bewildered as well by the vast quantities of trash coexisting in seeming harmony with great books. The mass-market paperback, originally born of some notion of bringing great books cheaply to a wide audience, had in fact flooded the country with silliness and countless new variations of genre junk, from yellow journalism to porn to how-to books. All issued like a mighty river from the puny spring of the Gutenberg-era slurs upon my countryman, Dracula. In principle, I could understand that in a democracy even trash has a right to a place in the sun. But the problems were immediately obvious: trash did not live side by side with great books. In most cases, it usurped them. Many great books were out of print or forgotten in America. Translations from world literature were spotty at best. I noticed many peculiar omissions. Trash sold much better than serious literature, and also tended to last longer on the shelves. I became acquainted for the first time with the notion of a "shelf life." The shelf life of a new book could be anywhere between three weeks and six months. Some vegetables last longer than that on supermarket shelves. My native notion of someone waiting desperately in an early morning line for books and vegetables contrasted oddly with the image of the throwaway book lasting less than a throwaway vegetable. I had to translate for myself the old distinction between literature and propaganda into a new one, the distinction between literature and trash.

In America, poetry, first novels, translations, and many other so-called literary books, if insufficiently sold, are not just pulled off the shelves: they are taken to a special place and destroyed. One such place is a factory in New Jersey where books are boiled in great big vats. The pulp of literature is then made back into inferior paper for shopping bags and advertising circulars. One stands before the great boiling vats of Jersey meditating on the fate of the carefully considered word. One of my books was boiled there, but it is not its fate that bewilders me (it deserved it). Think of all those boiling books and contrast that inflationary extravagance with the fact that in the Middle Ages a murderer could save his neck from hanging simply by being able to read. This was called "benefit of clergy," meaning that any man who could read had to be a clergyman, therefore outside the jurisdiction of a civil court, even if he had committed something as drastic as murder. In tracing the inflationary curve of literacy and the corresponding loss of awe toward the book, we are looking at a philosophical crux. At the point where inflation and rejection meet, a new player makes its appearance: the electronic eye.

The book, which began as reproductive propaganda, and which then prospered on fetishism and superstition, began to die from aesthetic attrition when it wasn't either pretty enough to worship or substantial enough to feed the increased appetite of an overstimulated population.

The epidemic of how-to books is a last-ditch effort to save the object by stressing its informational abilities. As data storage, however, the book is not very persuasive. Originally, practical-minded Americans must have wanted books that accessed "truth," whether spiritual or material, in clear terms. An anti-inflationary desire, no doubt, according to which novels and poems are no longer useful, but pointers on how to build a barn are. A computer, however, or a television program, is better with barn-building pointers. It stores, retrieves, and instructs quickly, and it can be slowed down or speeded up as needed.

To maintain itself distinct, a book then becomes interesting precisely when it *lacks pointers*, when it rejects absolutely the functions now better handled by electronics. The book becomes a different creature in the electronic age, it returns to its pre-Gutenberg function as a sacred object because it contains precisely what cannot be known by any other means. Walking a thousand miles to the next monastery (or small bookstore) becomes an act of faith in the *uniqueness* of the object. Television has not overthrown the book, it has merely overthrown Gutenberg. Paradoxically, then, the book has a great future, though not at the Center, which is now occupied by the electronic eye. After its millennium-long detour in the realm of center-making, the Gutenberg-era pamphlets on Dracula have come full circle. In that circle resides Western culture as we have known it. Outside it lies the pre- and post-Gutenberg book, a sacred poetic object which draws its power from its outsider position. On either side of the printed tales of Dracula lie the other versions of the same tales, the oral, handmade, incunabular, goldleafed, esoteric, one-of-a-kind objects. With each retelling, with each difficulty, the tales gain power. The mythical imagination gains hold in the approximate zones.

Where the printed book used to be—that is, at the center of the home—now stands a television set. Television has usurped only that aspect of the book that was most like itself, which did what TV itself does: replace direct vision with central programming. The book, in its centralizing role, had usurped the human capacity for adding, changing, inventing, remaking. It had become a Text, the Book, the Letter. As human beings grow more readily converted to efficiency they grow impatient with static objects, immutable verities; they crave mobility, flexibility, instantaneity.

Television is the book deconstructed for use into images, its moving parts. Yet words and images, though often convertible into each other, are essentially different modes of knowing.

The image is the enemy of the word: the two issue from different places, have different intentions, are located in different regions of the brain. For a thousand years the book was undoubtedly the most efficient means of storing and retrieving information. Its job was to create an interior for storing data, an expanding interior. This data was doomed to ambiguity, however, or to poetry, because words cannot be entirely contained. They leak around the referent, they spring into tales that are means of escape. The poetic tunnels lead out of the endless interiors books make. One of the lights at the end of one of these tunnels was in fact the bright glare of the television screen. Words streamed out of themselves to become images there. But there are other escapes, other tunnels, other lights, some of them completely unknown now, others beginning to be glimpsed.

In the dark country of my birth, these distant lights had been simply maddening. The official wall was everywhere riddled by these tunnels with pinpoints of light at their ends. The book was the only means of penetrating the profound darkness. Use of copying machines was strictly monitored for decades. Typewriter serial numbers had to be registered with the police. Print was endowed with a magic power, partly because the regime came to power through the printed word; its revolution had been the brainchild of the mimeograph machine. But in the December 1989 revolution, television occupied the center.

The first nationwide sign of trouble was booing at a Nicolae Ceausescu speech broadcast over state radio and television, which technicians tried to cover up with canned applause before "going to black." Ceauşescu then issued his "shoot to kill" order to local party bosses by closed circuit TV. His regime's public broadcasts were limited to two hours per night, and consisted entirely of propaganda; at his trial, Ceausescu said that he didn't want to tire out the people. A few days later, with perfect ironic symmetry that testifies either to the neutrality of the medium or to history's black sense of humor, Ceauşescu's own execution was aired over and over on the screens he once controlled. A friend told me how he'd been having a frightful time getting up for work after watching TV all night. The excitement on screen was nearly unbearable. Television literally woke up the country.

It was television unlike anything ever seen in the West, an outpouring of images that startled not just Romanians but the world. Being in the studios of Free Romanian Television on January 2 was one of the high points of my visit to revolutionary Romania. Studio Four, where the revolution had been in constant view since December 22, was the most heavily guarded building in Bucharest. The battle for the station had been one of the fiercest in the country. Young revolutionary guards with tricolor armbands had been sleeping and eating here since the beginning of the revolution. They feared that if they went home, the old Party hacks who were still around would seize the studio. A young woman who had been on the air twenty hours a day told me that she'd gone home only once—in a tank—to change clothes.

The extraordinary thing about what Romanians and the world (via CNN and French Television) were seeing on their screens was not just the sudden news and field reports, but the open invitation to the Romanian people to come and speak freely. Consequently, mobs of people milled in front of the tanks outside Studio Four, clamoring to get in with messages ranging from the profoundly serious to the profoundly silly. There were former political prisoners released from death row days before, and a thespian in the twilight of her years with a tape of poetry and music she hoped to recite and perform on television. A peasant from the region of Maramuresz talked for a full hour in vivid colloquialisms, and offered the country a fresh loaf of bread and a bottle of one hundred proof *tzuica*. The king of the Gypsies, the *boulibasha*, had his turn. When the flow of people slowed, the twenty-four-hour station aired things unseen and unheard-of in Romania: MTV videos stolen from satellites, and Italian and German soft porn. Romanians saw bare breasts on television for the first time in their history. As soon as someone established that I was a writer of Romanian origin (masquerading as an American journalist with National Public Radio), they put me on television as well; I mumbled my heartfelt good wishes.

The National Salvation Front of Romania—prompted by their rapt audience—instituted a series of reforms that often seemed improvised right in the studios: freedom of speech, opening of the borders, release of all political prisoners, five-day work week, landgrants to peasants, abolition of the death penalty, popular elections in the spring. The faces of the members of the Front and those of revolutionary guards running the station became utterly intermingled, so that some of the street fighters became leaders and were seen that way by millions of people. For a time, Romanian television was the central nervous system of the revolution. Gil Scott-Heron was, it seems, wrong when he said, "The revolution will not be televised." This revolution was *entirely* televised.

At its peak, Studio Four of Free Romania Television was an anarchic revolutionary medium. At the time of this writing, government spokespeople have already begun to allot time in a rational manner to sober parties. Aurel-Dragoş Munteanu, head of Romanian radio and TV, announced that after January 10, there would be a "formula for fair representation." The power of the medium is indisputable. Also indisputable is its "neutrality," its ability to reflect quickly and powerfully the interests of those who control it. The level of excitement generated by Romanian revolutionary television will be a great challenge to the programmers of the future. They will, doubtlessly, base their first generation of advertisements on the candor and sensuality of the revolution. Simulating the revolution, with its power to keep people awake, will one day be good business in Romania.

The distance between a place that fears words with preliterate fervor and a world that's having a postliterate price war on personal word processors is not measurable in geographical miles. West and East are the two points of a crescent connected by the electricity of the beginning and the end: the sizzling one hears is the agony of the word. At one point of the crescent is the old oral tradition (preliter- -ate, mythical, forbidden, tribal), and at the other point is the new oral tradition (postliterate, inescapable, global). Between them is the entire human library burning (or boiling).

We have put in books all the things we thought we might need to remember later. By removing this knowledge from our heads, we have made so many holes in the world that we now know nothing. Everything we know is in those boiling books. Our imaginations lost their connective weight, which is to say their sense of the world, when they abandoned so much in storage to the book. The library, our stored brain, was in actuality a spider gathering to itself all the threads that connected the things of this world to one another inside our minds.

Today in the West a person sits before a keyboard feeding his human interior into a machine's interior. His feeding of the new Center is no different from that of the Eastern European writer, feeding the blank page his imaginative responsibilities in the world. What *is* different is how the two exist and what the contents of the world they are feeding their respective centers into consist of. The respective consumers are different as well.

The reader is escaping *into* the world made by another human being. The reader's outside is the writer's inside and vice versa. Reading is a personal experience, the internalizing of another's world. The reader enters a world he stands apart from but which allows him to feel private, special, outside of himself. At the same time, the experience of reading is dynamic and personal: communication occurs through osmosis. The book preserves the notion of a divine origin, even as it delivers its reader to the demonic centralism that will eventually empty him. The Writer and the Reader, both creatures of the word, have been present since creation and they are indispensable to the demiurgic act. The word needs to be witnessed in order to be.

In the West, the Reader, once privy to the act of creation, has become the Spectator, the Viewer, the Consumer of the Image. The Reader and the Viewer are not the same creature: if they once had the same origin, they are now two competing strains of humanity. The Viewer is a more docile creature than the Reader: he allows himself to be manipulated both by the sources of the image before which he sits, fingers poised above the keyboard, and by the end result of the image, which is the command to produce and consume more images. Very little of the secret arrogance of the privileged Reader survives in the Viewer. The book encourages individuality in its dual and opposing roles as internalizer and liberator. The private act of reading is an incitement against collective mentality. The image, on the other hand, exists to be shared by all.

The image bears no more resemblance to reality than does the word, but it does not *appear* so. It seems to us that the image is more intimate with reality. After all, our memories recognize the shapes of the real in the image more readily than in the word. This illusion has thoroughly seduced us. Images, however, are not reality: they are simulacra. Successful simulacra. We have now reached the point in the capitalist West where the simulacra have taken hold and are actively eliminating reality. The simulacra may in fact have already become reality. In the real world there isn't room enough for all the people. But they all fit in the unreal world, the one made by images. The difficulty of distinguishing between the illusions of commodity culture and reality haunt the art of our time. Memory, never very reliable, is easily fooled. The copy cannot be told from the original. When the memory of the "real" goes, the image may not even bear much resemblance to the original. The conceit will have become obsolete. We will live in an abstract world (if we don't already). The real will have become strictly mythical. We won't notice the disappearance of the Outside, or our lack of desire for it. The attenuation and eventual disappearance of *place* leads to the attenuation and eventual disappearance of desire. Having the illusion of everything leaves one wanting nothing. The illusion of depth is just that: an illusion. The image is flat, one-dimensional, though it can thoroughly confuse the senses. Not knowing anything intimately (that is, dimensionally) leads to the loss of desire to perpetuate it. Why want something without *depth?* Love penetrates/is penetrated, can only manifest in depth. This sad state of affairs may already be far advanced, which makes it all the more urgent to introduce the mythical into the everyday, or to disrupt, at least, its march. The conquest of the West by the image is partly a victory for surrealist nightmares, partly the wedge of a new world breaking through the crust of the old one. Iconography has become the ideology of our time.

The image is both the earlier and the later stage of the word. The word began as pictograph to synthesize images. It became an edict to suppress them. It is an image again. The word was a seed in the fruit of the image. It embodied

Time, and assured the transmission and continuity of a shared agreement. The word was a critique of the image. The pulp surrounding it was round, timeless, simultaneous, and it held around the core. The word negotiated a tenuous understanding between mystery and our social survival. This tenuous agreement, like the Khyber Pass, is the focus of all ambition. Power is the ability to control the traffic of signs between word and world.

In *illo tempore* no one spoke. But immediately after, in the age of demigods and heroes, poetry controlled the narrow pass. Religion then took the job, followed closely by philosophy, then by print journalism. In the newspapers, the word ended. The last word was in the last edition. The seed dissolved in the flesh and the fruit exploded in a billion images.

Unlike the word, the image bypasses entirely the question of judgment. The image cannot be adjudicated. One cannot resist its authority by means of morality because it so resembles the world its morality appears intrinsic. It simply takes over. Unlike the word, it need not follow a complex grammar. Its language is the flow: it can be sequential or simultaneous. Insofar as the image is sequential, it is a kind of writing, but it need not concern itself with literacy. Everyone is image-literate. The paucity of Commie images (billions of little heads of Lenin) and the lack of color account for the slowness of Soviet society to partake in the computer-imaged interior of the millennium. The populations of the Soviet states are still *masses,* in that word-heavy, undifferentiated, trudging way. The interior they inhabit is that of the cell, of the word. The image-mediated interiority of the West is euphoric because it creates the illusion of open-endedness, simultaneity, possibility. The image appropriates the Outside. Those are trees on TV but the breeze feels good. The inside *looks* like the Outside, and there is nothing in the vast amnesiac present to compare it to except (now) incomprehensible word pictures in old books. But if you've never seen a tree, no words will make it real for you. The image will make it, if not real, then "real." All images belong. There are no out-of-place images, no incongruities. Surrealism is the real language of images. We become instantly bored with any deliberately logical buildup of images. The image subdued by narrative reverts to the word; it becomes recognizable, boring. Illustrating words with images is a transitional hangover from the age of the word. True image-speech is surrealist. Collage is its basic articulation.

The image is accessible; it does not need a cumbersome grammar to constitute itself into a language; it is entirely welcoming to other images; its connections are always open; it is infinitely modular. It gives itself up to other images to become a different image. It is a constant conspiracy of inclusion. The big picture, the cosmic scheme, is inherently present. The universe is symmetrical as is all order, natural or imaginary. The State is a symmetrical bit of the symmetrical universe. Our biology is correspondingly symmetrical. There is geometry in the universe. Micro- and macrocosm are harmonic and, what's more, obvious. The image possesses the evidence of obviousness. Our eyes service the image. Without the critical responses of other senses, the eyes are limitless consumers of images. The rise of the image corresponds to a diminishment of the other senses.

The only articulate unease about this unprecedented conquest of reality by representation has come from artists. When Salvador Dali and Luis Buñuel put a razor blade through an eye in *Un Chien Andalou,* they were putting an X through the image. Ironically, the image itself did not protest. It was in a movie. The eyes are the most unprotesting sense of the body. A basket full of luscious tomatoes slides into view on the shopping channel on cable TV. Look, a ripe but firm rose-tinted pear. You shop with your eyes, not with your fingers. Your nose has no say in it. You can't put it to your cheek to see how it feels. The eyes have it.

The other senses are in exile. The nose, running out of things to smell, begins to shrink. The vast tactile sea that used to cover the skin and peak in the fingertips is drying up. The taste buds flee the tongue like little migrating birds, leaving it good only for wagging. Cravings, unchecked by the play of senses, grow enormous. The eyes set no limits to desire. They speak directly to the pleasure centers. Production can barely keep up with the demand stimulated by images. Advertising today does not attempt to sell products as much as to create a special type of consumer for each image advertised. It thus limits demand and creates new social distinctions, classes whose differences are based not on wealth or birth but on imaginary differences among products.

One must *earn the right to buy* certain things. Eventually, there will be numerous consumer classes, distinguished only by their controlled cravings. Special "crave meters" attached to their wrists will compute the quantity of advertising they have absorbed to see if they are worthy of the product. The "reader" will correlate credit with possibility. If craving exceeds balance it will calculate likely future earnings, and if the human unit looks unlikely to pay for its desires the human will be terminated. Future beings will have smooth heads, without mouths or noses. Two huge eyes perpetually fixed on the endless movie will relay a sense of superiority to each unit to make it ready to die for what it craves.

The surrealist global village is here. Shopping is possible, despite time differences, everywhere. The clock by which markets open and close regulates the rhythm of belonging. Anyone can arrive in any part of the global village without turning. For each departure and arrival the clock adjusts the picture. The vantage point remains constant. One travels inside calculated differences in precise sync with all the other differences. Traffic is destiny. From inside the assigned difference one can comment on the passing landscape, which is always the same.

Only in the Third World (national peripheries) and in the artistic peripheries (in exile and native) does the image still encounter resistance. There are vivid memories of a cosmos consisting of a different body, a body of stories and songs. The meanings of earth, sky, and human are available in ways specific only to that particular place. But here, too, images, backed by the World Bank and by tourism, are reordering the world.

A complicated tradition defines the native. As representatives of the colonial world that first brought natives the clock (and Western armies), tourists are the civilian inspectors. They are here to ensure the proper passing of the symbolic order into artifact making, of ritual into entertainment. They come before and after the armies, first with their sketchbooks, then with their cameras, to position the natives in the big picture (composed of all their montaged little photos). The armies do the physical job. The tourists do the metaphysical one.

Soon enough natives *see* themselves in the big picture. Still, the tourist must spot-check constantly. The pull of tradition in many places exceeds the pull of TV and must be caught by the click of the shutter. Stubborn differences can be montaged to fit. The machinery can absorb anything, but the edges must be smooth. There must be fittings. The places where tourists and natives rub together are where the fittings occur. The juice of *seeing* soon flows through the newly joined bodies. Blood is then replaced by photons. When the blood is all drained, the native dies and becomes himself the tourist. He views himself from the Outside: he has been trapped in the picture and is now looking back from a superior distance. The new tourist-native takes his brand-new corpse on a great journey of *seeing* around the newly conquered and soon-to-be-televised wilderness and tries to shove others through the eye of the camera. All enter the narrow circle of the camera lens, never to return: the Outside will be only a memory now. The circle of the camera eye squeezes tighter, pushing the former natives through narrower and narrower circles. They are crawling like miners under the surface of a world that used to be theirs. They are miners, digging out the psychic coal for their new master, The Picture. The natives now see what the tourist sees because they are one. The global village is a large corpse connected by electricity to its own objectification. The part that *sees* is the central part. The part that resists is the remnant of the human. In the global village no one leaves home because home is everywhere.

The Triumphant Shipwreck of Dada and Surrealism

> What is admirable about the fantastic
> is that there is no longer anything fantastic:
> there is only the real. Experience itself has
> found itself increasingly circumscribed. It
> paces back and forth in a cage from which it
> is more and more difficult to make it
> emerge.
>
> —André Breton, *Manifesto of Surrealism*

Vindicated prophets are not happy people. The hells-to-come they once described arrive at last and swallow them. The major problem of prophecy has always been the circumvention of hell in order to arrive at the good times that lie beyond it. In the past, so-called prophets of doom, from Isaiah to Allen Ginsberg, have tarried unseemingly long in the pits of darkness before surrendering to the inevitable light. I have always suspected prophets of enjoying the things they abhor and abjure because it is only through them that they can rise to heights sufficient for loosening their rhetorical lightning.

Today, the problem of the prophet has been solved—eliminating, alas, the prophet. No sooner does the vision make its tingling appearance than the corresponding reality comes quickly in sight, before even a proper taste of doom.

This is the fate of prophets in today's global village: they are right no matter what they prophesy. Things and their opposites lie together in the beam of the projector we dust motes dance in. Who solved the prophet's problem while depriving him of the pleasure of giving us hell? Who had the nerve to be convinced before the proper harangue even began? What kind of world is this where utopia's there for the taking, whether it be a microwave heaven or holy death by Iraqi gas?

Surrealists have some of the answers. They foresaw, in the 1920s and 1930s, the growing importance of Seeing. Not "sight," that immobile noun pinned to the lapel of high culture, but the active act of "seeing," the axis about which Western civilization revolves at increasing speeds. Since involuntarily blind Homer and willfully blind Oedipus, the eyes have been looming larger and larger in the stone forehead of the West. During Enlightenment "seeing" became synonymous with knowledge and conquest. To see the unknown was to possess it. From the microscope to the telescope, the microcosm and the macrocosm, our effort has been to encompass the unseen by the seen. That which was seen was then destroyed by the dissecting gaze before it could return it. The unknown, pinned by the gaze of the knower, shriveled under the taxonomic light of marching sight. Prophecy, the art of seeing the future, became just one more extension of visual conquest. Human organizations as old as the species were overthrown one by one by the giddiness that accompanied the tearing of the veils. Even their memory, belonging as it did to "ages of darkness," was obscured by the marching light.

But then—a "then" culminating in World War I— something paradoxical began to occur with alarming frequency. There were tremendous lapses in the steady progress of light. War irrupted ferociously in the newly lit world of reason, more destructive and apocalyptic than ever prophesied. The quality of the darkness tearing the fabric of the enlightened world was of an impenetrable density. A malignant darkness, infinitely more potent than the benign terrors of the ancient night or of "the primitive soul," began to make its appearance. After World War I our faith in reason was never restored. Artists flocked to the irrational. The eyes became suspect, seeing was doubted, and a new adventure of the human spirit began. The Dadaists composed with their eyes closed, listening only for the discordant signals that alone seemed to hold an understanding. Logic, rhetoric, reason, closure, beauty, harmony were put on trial. They belonged to the blithe ages of mindless sight. The various monsters awakened when their protective darkness had been removed by science now stood at attention. They had shapes other than classical, and they were gazing at us. At that point, it occurred to quite a few startled souls that our orgy of voyeurism had stirred the lust of whatever is just behind the mirror. And it was *looking back!* Reason began a desperate and hasty campaign to shrink the Outside at that point by definitively ridding the world of myth, religion, the supernatural—in short, whatever was not us.

Quickly, psychoanalysis pointed inside and located all the monsters in the unconscious. Why, they were nothing but repressed sexual desires. Marxism found the demons hidden in the forces of production, veritable supervisor-devils in the factory of history. Art began to depict a world unlike the one received by our eyes. The new things it showed us had been ours all along, residing in the imagination, of course. The imagination, while roomier than the unconscious (it contained things that didn't exist as well as repressed ones!) and less regimented than the factory of history, was the best corral yet: monsters could roam there in all their dimensions! Grammarians discovered the self-referentiality of language. All those scary words! They had only been playing with each other since the beginning of time, meaning nothing by it. Language became both immanent and material, an infinite maze where the wandering monsters would be lost. Following the cue of grammarians, the sciences fell in love with their grammars as well, each one an autonomous world. Structuralism transformed all the little rooms of knowledge into traps for the monsters of the Outside. Thus a new world came into being: one in which humans contain monsters because they are neurotic, imagine the unimaginable because they are artists, are oppressed because of their class, use language because it gives them more language.

This rapid deployment of defenses, it was hoped, would spare us from the Outside which, anyway and most probably, did not exist. And even if it did, at least we might contain it, making it the Formerly Outside by marrying it. The Formerly Outside would be smaller and once we got it all inside we could control it. The shrunken monsters would soon resign themselves to being mere appendages of our fancy. These ostrich-like tactics must have mightily amused the recently aroused demons. You can hear them laughing today in Iran, Baton Rouge, Israel, Beirut, India, and Africa.

André Breton was an optimist. So were most of the surrealists, though many of them committed suicide. Surrealist optimism was based on the possibility of a complete transformation of human beings through radical "conservation" and through the return of the repressed. The overthrow of the acquiescent human being was an intoxicating proposition. The surrealists proposed to do this through a thorough critique of reason, installing in its place the discarded (suppressed) discourses of dream and fantasy. If logic is the language of machines, dream is the language of humans. The surrealists advocated the rending of the veils of reason. Before reason had both stripped and obscured it, the unknown had been the true home of human beings. The tearing of the veils, the lifting of the curtain, the shifting of the gears, the tearing of the skin, the lifting of the skirt, the shifting of the eyes, the tearing of the skirt from the shifting of the eyes to the lifting of the curtain, all these and all their potential erotico-linguistic displacements constituted a kind of marvel of anti-engineering, perfectly feasible in the great mechanical workshop of the West which had so far produced only the destroying gaze.

The surrealist antimachine produced two antidotes to the march of formulas: the Marvelous and its companion, Laughter, solidarity-building laughter, laughter that cut the Gordian knot, paradox-solving and paradox-making laughter. The Marvelous was the chief substance, though, and its producers were those discarded by the official production machine: marginal beings, peripheral souls, dream operators, poets, but eventually everyone. Surrealist Humor would cause a liberating rippling of the Scale of Mirth, from the slight grin of Huysmans' Des Esseintes to the rippling proletarian guffaws of Fantomas, and Surrealist Wonder would create a new human being and a community based on inspiration, not ideology. Property relations would certainly be affected as well as the demons of production. The surrealists separated the images of things from the things themselves and intended these images to be more than mere things, to be inspirational chariots. The key to advancing creation was an unbounded imagination. How to liberate it was the question in modern society. The surrealists demanded the taking down of the corral fences of the imagination, the opening of the borders between the human and the nonhuman, the monstrous and the domestic. It was a tall order in a world where, said Breton, the "imagination which knows no bounds is . . . allowed to be exercised only in strict accordance with the laws of an arbitrary utility; it is incapable of assuming this inferior role for very long and, in the vicinity of the twentieth year, generally prefers to abandon man to his lusterless fate."

Man without imagination was a plaything of forces indeed. Madness was one solution to the prospect of a hideously dull existence, others were dreams, *écriture automatique*, hypnosis, exploration of the psyche, the study of magic, psychotropic drugs. Antonin Artaud was both mad and a taker of drugs. Henri Michaux took mescaline. The surrealists differed from the Romantics, their predecessors, only by the texture of the world they lived in. The modern world's machine had put Nature, which the Romantics still had nearly unmediated access to, out of reach. The wilderness of the eighteenth century had pretty much become a park by the twentieth. Consequently, both imagination and nature had become more difficult to come by: the way to both our inner and our outer Outside was piled high with the debris of civilization.

The surrealists investigated our inner wilderness with the help of Dr. Freud's unconscious. This unconscious was something that had been found by Dr. Freud not long before Breton was born, under old family photos in the Biedermeier trunk of old Vienna. All the rejecta of history and the flora and fauna of bourgeois dreams inhabited this place. It was as rich a place as anyone would dare to imagine, and it was there for the taking, at the beck and call of a linguistic mechanism called *écriture automatique*, automatic writing. The surrealist *écriture automatique* differed from "free association" only in the order that analysis imposed on the things brought to light. Analysis deemed order necessary to reintegrate the individual into society. The surrealists deemed disorder equally necessary in order *to critique* society. Nonetheless, the apparent complexity of both operations led to complicity between surrealism and psychoanalysis to create and legitimize the psychoanalytic profession. The compact must have originally contained an equal clause for the creation of a professional surrealist, something that didn't come to pass until much later, until now, that is. There is a touch of *la belle époque* here, like Freud's neatly trimmed beard.

Automatic writing is antiverbal: it uses words to bring out images. Free association, on the other hand, is anti-image: it is an organizer of images into words. The images resulting from automatic writing destroy the orderly subduing of consciousness to the rules of society. The images subsumed by the words of the sentence give up their ghost to the syntax. Surrealism creates chaos; psychoanalysis creates order. For all that, the surrealists were intimately connected to bourgeois Europe, both as thinkers and as Parisians: they were city bohemians, adversaries of art in a world of art, outsiders by vocation, insiders in actuality. Psychoanalysis, born out of Central Europe also, proclaimed its allegiance to civilization: it was an intentional insider but its activity was international, possibly supranational. Both surrealism and psychoanalysis helped internationalize and eventually delocalize human beings, but each did so in spite of their professed aims. By supporting each other's aspirations, the two methods also wrote each other's death warrants. Psychoanalysis, the religion of the word, was absorbed by surrealism, the religion of the image, but not until the word played itself out in modern Europe. There was a kind of *politesse* in their transaction, an opening-of-the-doors ritual: first psychoanalysis, which was allowed to close the modern era, then surrealism, which took the end of verbal discourse out the same door. Then they parted ways. Psychoanalysis went off to dissolve in the inflation of the word and surrealism disappeared in the proliferation of moving icons. The small politeness of succession was all that was left of the old European contract between words and images. After the manners were performed, the signs took over, leaving their old meanings behind like empty insect cases.

Where is the unconscious today? Freud invented it. Jung populated it with weird Germanic phantoms he called archetypes. The surrealists made it a place for poets, like a café in the shadow of Tour St. Jacques. Criminals used it in court. Worst of all, men with pointy beards made money out of it, and filled the vacuum left by the death of the Catholic confession. It also gave Jews a taste of Catholicism, like pork that didn't come from a pig. The unconscious was a boon to the barely educated, too. By having it there, at the bottom or behind everything—who can say where?—one could always console oneself with the knowledge that if something emotionally strong was ever needed, it could be opened up (with qualified help!) to have a "long draught of darkness," a psychic whiskey, as it were. For three-quarters of a century it was a populous place. A gold mine, a bottomless pit, a chunk of language attached to something many experts could attest to.

Where did it go? The fact is that the unconscious is gone. According to a psychoanalyst of my acquaintance, every attempt to penetrate below the surface these days produces nothing but television jingles. To his request to say anything that comes to mind, his patients now say: "It's not nice to fool Mother Nature." Asked how he is feeling, the patient replies: "The more you look the more you like." The earliest thing he remembers? "Reach out and touch someone." Identity crisis? "You're in the Pepsi generation." "I wish I were an Oscar Meyer wiener!" What does he want from life? "Double your pleasure, double your fun." Questioning the primal things, he gets: "G. E. brings good things to life." It isn't just that the history of television populates the ontological pipeline. It is as if there are no more individual secrets: they seem to have all melted into one huge secret, now in the keeping of the military-industrial-entertainment complex, instead of the Oedipal one.

There is no point in regretting the passing of the unconscious. We are a new kind of being now: we don't need an unconscious, we *are* unconscious.

America is de facto surrealist. There is no need to upset "reality" here. "Reality" is manufactured continually. The incongruous meeting of different realities is a routine matter. People inhabit the landscape at angles so odd they would surely fall if a continually evolving projection machinery weren't constantly correcting the perspective. It was only natural that the European unconscious, so structurally well furnished, would meet its demise here where the huddled masses of the nineteenth century came to eat. America was the projection of European utopias, a heaven on earth very much like that of Charles Fourier, who believed that the pear was the most noble fruit and whom the surrealists adopted as an adequate counterweight to Christian futurism and fatalism. America was the last hope of European revolutionaries, the Outside par excellence.

The Victorian upper class did not like America. They found it rude, awesome, and unmanageable. By its very presence it denied the miniaturized order of the Old World. In England, the interior went outside; in America, the outside came in. The English lawn was a carpet, the American table a tree stump. To British writer Frances Trollope, Niagara Falls was "an accompaniment to conversation." Or it was a marvel of technical efficiency: "So much over so sheer a drop," and "power of eye control is necessary for full enjoyment of the scenery." Oscar Wilde said about Niagara Falls: "The sight of the stupendous waterfall must be one of the first, if not the keenest, disappointments in American married life."

In the process of observing America, many writers

concluded that traditional writing forms were made obsolete by the new social and psychological configurations of
the New World. Having decided on the "novel's irrelevance
to America," many of them looked for alternative forms:
Kipling's epic, Stevenson's chivalric romance, Wells's and
Huxley's science fiction were invented specifically to accommodate the new. It is curious, then, that American
literature until Whitman stayed so closely and timidly in the
shadow of the Queen's English. Even in the 1920s, when
surrealism seduced many Americans in Paris, the echoes of
that revolution were only faint in America. It is even more
curious when one considers that surrealism was in the main
an optimistic movement (in both its conservative and its
subversive modes), and America is the only place in the
world where optimism has been legislated, by making the
"pursuit of happiness" a right. All utopians were avant-
Americans, and if Columbus hadn't found the place, all
those utopians would have had to go to the moon with Jules
Verne.

Small utopian communities functioned in America since
its founding. The utopian enterprise of the 1960s was in the
suppressed tradition of countless utopian experiments of
the nineteenth century. These communities were pressured
out of existence but not before giving America the forms of
its future. Their ecological concerns, their belief in crafts, in
human-scale industry, became the legacy on which the
antitechnological revolt of our time is founded. There are
those who argue, like Jackson Lears in *No Place of Grace:
Antimodernism and the Transformation of American Culture,
1880–1920,* that what began as an antimodern revolt ended
up revitalizing the modern. This is true but only in a formal
sense: the contentless images changed the "look," just as the
hippie "look" fed yuppie commerce and surrealism feeds
MTV. Forms are forever migrating out of that which has
created them to become used against it. Aren't the rebellious

anthems of the 1960s now used to sell soap on TV?

On the other hand, the revelation of seams between images, caught at the moment of leaving one content to be captured by another, and the increasing speed at which these decantings take place, make American sense in a kind of everyday working way. Far from being provoked to fits of deliberate intellectual eccentricity, the average TV watcher here can go straight from Carmen Miranda's hat to a cameo appearance by Sigmund Freud on "Fantasy Island" to a bathtub filled with strangers in the middle of the city, and then drive off to work making cobalt bombs. Does he realize the contradictions as Dada and therefore inevitably absurd, or as surrealist and therefore holding great occult and utopian meaning? Both. The continued existence (and relevance) of Dada is a religious phenomenon. Absurdity is the chief demon of capitalism, the material of endless "situation comedies." The absurd and the occult star side by side in every debate. For those unable to digest them in the abstract, there are supermarket tabloids. Aliens land continually. We are both in awe of the industrial Moloch and in dread of what, if anything, it stands for, or in the way of. Thus both one's "situation" (comic and episodic) and one's fate after death ("the soul") are constantly under consideration. Most electronic signals beamed at the mass carry "situational" and "metaphysical" messages. Can one participate in this kind of discussion? No. It is conducted through us. Which leaves the "real" world (the will to the Outside) in the hands of *agents provocateurs*. The Dadaistic perception can thus become the stimulus for a wicked, terminal kind of fun (techno-sense intended), yielding of poetic explosions and sensual derangement grander than geography. But, alas, it still delivers the amnesiac practitioner directly into the arms of the commodity. The religious, B-movie–inspired science of perversity and meticulous investigation that surrealism demands is forgotten in Dada. Dada holds on to the thing (even in the simulacra: it suspects that the body's in the trunk), while surrealism holds on to the image (whose job is to assist the simulacra in disposing of the body). What is left of the romantic nineteenth century in people struggles between these poles of surrealist production ("fun") and Dada consumption ("lifestyle").

As surrealist images become the signature of our *fin-de-siècle*, surrealist writings sink into oblivion. Postmodernists are embarrassed by the revolutionary roots of surrealism. The surrealist spirit of insurgency is still active but it had to be purged from the literature of the inside that succeeded it. *Écriture automatique* is still a threat because it assumes the unlimited potential of the imagination against the given facts of modern life. There is no doubt that many of the images liberated by early surrealist *écriture automatique* are now mere advertising emblems. But the surrealists themselves never put much store in the finished products of their insurgent methods. The familiar surrealist forms became an archival enterprise but not the deliberate pursuit of the irrational. Recorded dreams became a bore but dreams remain interesting to the dreamer. The object is to become not involuntary analysts or recorders but active dreamers.

There is a quaint remnant of orthodox surrealism today that labors under the illusion that the politics and world of the 1930s are eternal. This leftover ideology goes against the surrealist spirit and accomplishes precisely what surrealists hoped would never happen, namely, their becoming "literature," their "revolution of the word" no more than another historical thingamajig in the long succession of "isms"—realism, impressionism, expressionism, and so on. Surrealist techniques of investigation and weapons are perfectly ambiguous in today's world: they can be read and used in diametrically opposed ways. Collage, for instance, is both a literary (or painterly) technique that shifts context to reveal something new and the dominant mode of visual control in the language of advertising and the media.

Likewise Dada. When Tristan Tzara proposed making a poem from a newspaper randomly cut up, he was offering an alternative to the literature of reason. He freed the words: he returned language to its potential state. Tzara de-bourgeoisified language by taking it out of the hands of perspective-makers. It was a revolution executed through the simple erasure of grammar and its tricks of meaning. The possibility that once words were detached from their grammatical jobs of policing bourgeois interests the world might once again become visible has not lost its appeal. A similar intention animated the painters who had begun dismantling realism even before Dada. But unbeknownst to them, the revolutionary Dadaists were also enriching the store of art where the future was already shopping. They were multiplying the materials. Tzara opened a hole in the hull of literature—he was the iceberg—hoping that reality would leak in. Instead, everything came to help itself to the new stuff of the imagination. That particular boat has now suffered hasty patching at the hands of any number of philosophies of art, as well as severe entombment in museums. Nonetheless, the vessel sails on, exceedingly vulnerable, at the mercy in fact of any passing Dadaist. The method works even if the patched holes have been neutralized by having them pass for art. Museums, to extend the metaphor, are where the patched holes can be viewed.

If we face a new situation today, it is the speed with which everything is copied, co-opted, and turned against itself. The original of anything, whether it be a poem or an assassination, still preserves something of the freshness of the intent. No such freshness will be found in the copy. And the copy of the copy will have long turned its energy against the very freshness that spawned its ancestor. The simulacrum hatches in our lack of attention. It feeds in the dark of this lack on the relative rigidity of ideas until it disposes of the substance (which is everything but the resemblance to the original). (Are there simulacra, one wonders, that have disposed even of the resemblance? Proudly original copies? Robots that have designed themselves?) The disposed-of substance undergoes a reprimalization and escapes into the Outside whose substance it is and where it awaits the formalizing forays of the next explorers. Images do not have ideology, nor do they have a definite place of origin. Their *materia prima*, the Outside, is, however, always ready to send its projections along the lines of ideas and images. What activates the Outside is power. The Greeks, who authored our civilization, did so by harnessing the Outside. Gilles Deleuze notes, "What the Greeks did is not to reveal Being or unfold the Open in a world-historical gesture. According to Foucault, they did a great deal less, or more. They bent the Outside, through a series of practical exercises. . . . Force is what belongs to the Outside, since it is essentially a relation between other forces: it is inseparable in itself from the power to affect other forces (spontaneity) and to be affected by others (receptivity). But what comes about as a result *is a relation which force has with itself, a power to affect itself, an affect of self on self.*" Thus the Greeks, unlike the showy nomads of the sweeping gesture, achieved the mastery of the Outside through *repetition.* Which does not mean that they then trapped the Outside inside their grammar, availing themselves of its force. The structures contain only models, traps, techniques—which have been getting better and better, culminating in the relentless ability for repetition of the machine.

Machines repeat. It is their Greek job. There is no conflict in the apparent (inside) world between Fordianism and surrealism. The assembly line is capable of producing infinite quantities of things, including surrealists, and providing enough Dadaists to shadow them. It is not even a matter of demand. The market is the lifetime of the machine, which is practically eternal. The market is always the exact size of the production. As long as the machine churns, the market supports it. In the process, what used to be known as a human being stretches to make room in itself for the products. After stretching, it splits, and each schizo fragment walks away with its new load of production. And so on. Assembly-line artists are at work "on themselves," cultivating the increasing appetites of divided self which is itself in great demand for the market. Their job is to produce an infinitely reproduceable self capable of consuming all the simulacra spewing out of the repetitions of the machine. Surely the surrealist eye is pleased, even as the surrealist spirit recoils. The horror of art that surrealist art conveyed was the horror of the surrealist vision coming through in an everyday sort of way. Surrealist art now hangs in museums, safely jailed from its own vision. Its escaped "images" issue nonstop from the electronic center. The surrealist explorer of the unconscious has been replaced by the unconscious surrealist.

Americans are horrified by the arbitrary, no matter that if they really looked around them they would find little that is not. Which is why surrealism never took hold here. Surrealist techniques were modified so that they would seem "useful," in the manner of garage projects. Take, for instance, Cut-up, the American version of the Dada poem.

William Burroughs and Brion Gysin, who began cutting up texts in the 1950s, were not interested in completely dismantling "meaning," as had been Tzara's suggestion. They wanted to enlarge both the area of use and the area of sense. They believed that secrets lay hidden below the surface meanings held in place by grammar: suppressed heresies, conspiracies, webs of control. Their Anglo-American steadfastness refused to believe in the obviousness of the first control level as evidenced by bourgeois writing. In the area of use they wanted a large compost heap, a huge available store, made up of all the words and sounds in popular and arcane use, including slang, newspapers, tape-recorded conversation, other languages: convertible capital for future works. In fact, while some of their cut-ups remained just that, many were mined by Burroughs later for his novels. In the area of sense, Cut-up had an experimental, mechanical intention. Mr. Burroughs from Kansas, an heir of the adding machine, took language apart in his garage not because it was the same apart as it was whole, and not because it was better dismantled, and not because the dismantling act was joyous in itself (though certainly there was plenty of fun in it!), but because he wanted to see if by *rearranging* the parts he could not somehow make the thing *work differently*. His intentions were not philosophical: they were experimental. Unlike those easily transcendent Europeans always ready to take their case Outside, Americans are practical: "No ideas but in things." (I'll come back to that later.)

What did Gysin and Burroughs discover? On the immediate level they saw that if you cut up the Bible, Shakespeare, Rimbaud, they were still the Bible, Shakespeare, and Rimbaud. But in every case, *there was a little left over*. What? A new sentence here and there, full of an odd sense. A prophetic sentence, for instance: "It is a bad thing to sue your own father"; "And there is a horrid air conditioner." These things, says Burroughs, have nothing to do with the text being cut up. They are about the person doing the cut-up. After building a store of these "messages," Burroughs extended the process to some of his machine familiars. He asks, How many times do you hear a sentence just *stand out* of context to speak to *you*? The radio'll be breezing along, and suddenly there is a message: "Bill, you must polish your wings." Everywhere sentences stand out of their referential contexts to address us directly. They jump out of texts, radios, and other so-called objective media. One doesn't have to be schizophrenic to hear these messages. But one may have to make oneself schizophrenic in order to pay attention. That is, if one isn't already "spontaneously" schized by the market. There is hardly a need for intention in order to become many in America. Rimbaud's "one makes oneself a seer by the complete derangement of the senses," is status-quo–activated, radio blaring, all channels open. For the purposes of discovering hidden meaning cut-up is only a tool, not necessary after one becomes adept at turning over the soil of messaging. A writer will find the unexpected in his own work when he rereads it: sentences he hasn't written, sentences that have radically changed meaning, sentences stuck into the writing by invisible hands while he slept. Burroughs insists that channels other than the ones officiated over by Oedipal/State amnesia actually exist. How about the "little voice in your ear," he asks, "the one that told you to do it"?

Uncovering what these voices tell is "the Job." These voices with their special directions and private language are a separate and deliberately suppressed part of the overall voice of the world. This part will stand up for you if you can split it from the main bloc of noise to make it rise into your ear. What's more, the better you listen, the more you hear it. It's in everything: in the howl of the wind, the barking of dogs, the clanging of machines. The oppressive chattering of the world is corrected and defeated by this operation. With some luck, it can be muted: certain devices are now capable of removing "white" noise. Grown-ups don't hear voices because they hear the Voice. But children and outsiders do, because they cannot afford not to. It is the Job.

The Outside is in these voices. Useful language is not

made out of thoughts or feelings or ideas but out of little voices. Furthermore, one cannot simply pick up the little voices but should *provoke* them into being, in a sportslike manner, to see how many can be scared up in one day, in one hour, in one minute. Burroughs's voices bring up the related matter of hearing and mishearing. Like the Dadaists, but for different reasons again, he advocates mishearing. Instead of hearing what one knows is there, one must choose to hear something different, something new, something that isn't there. Mishearing is the true aristocrat of hearing. By extension, so are mistakes. How far into a new truth can one be taken by mistakes? "Never let a typo go," Ted Berrigan advised me, "it may be the threshold of the new, the door into the unexpected." Mishearing. Mistakes. Misunderstanding. Misgivings. Miscasting. All the pretty misses of discovery.

So where are we in the square garage of midwestern American experiment? In exactly the same place the Dadaists and surrealists were in their smoky café. The difference perhaps is that Europeans are unabashedly transcendental, while Americans have scruples. I have come to prefer garage transcendentalism to the other kind because I like the tinkering. But when I get really going I jump on my hat.

Pop art provides another commentary on the shipwreck (or victory) of Dada/surrealism in North America. Instead of producing a great big store full of stuff, pop art looks at the world as a great store already, from which it is possible to select one or two choice items, a can of soup or a lipstick, reframing or rephrasing them as "art" and recirculating them at a higher (market) value. Its vantage point has shifted from that of the producer to that of the consumer. The question of meaning, which is the enemy of Dada, and the schizofied goal of Cut-up, does not arise at all. A new obviousness is in the world. Pop art is not a greedy consumer of things; it is aristocratic, anorexic. It despises all things except those lit by caprice. Like Cyrano it wants only one grape. Like Cyrano it'll make a big deal out of it. Meaning becomes the amusement of manipulating a purchase. The Dadaists smashed the furniture of meaning and were haunted by what they had rejected: debris followed them around. They tried to make this ectoplasm disappear but the only available nothingness was the lack of distinction between meaningful and meaningless language. Meaning for the Dada was real: a bourgeois definition made out of words for the uses of power. Meaning and lack of meaning were made to exchange places until the labored conclusion of their arbitrariness was drawn: the law was made relative.

Cut-up cared about neither amusement nor relativity. On the contrary, it sought meaning. Scholastic, almost medieval, it fiddled with the technology in the garage hoping to restore the meaning relativized by the Dadaists and made gauche by pop art. Burroughs and Gysin used the tape recorder because they could manipulate time better by fast-forwarding and playback. The machinery of control, composed of contracts the structures of power have buried into the language, was easily discernible by manipulating time. A good example of this is "backward masking," which involves playing tape backwards until a counter-meaning emerges. Burroughs's recorder picked up Hitler, Nietzsche, and Goethe among the generalized babble of the dead, when he left the machine running at night. It is irrelevant whether these voices actually belonged to these dead eminences, because they were in fact there, could be put in books, as Burroughs indeed did, in *Last Words of Dutch Schultz* and *The Wild Boys*. He approached the voices like a detective: deducing from them the secret messages intended for privileged communication. He used ordinary reality as a kind of grid to lay on top of the wild babble to make out the code. This is the way the National Security Agency grids all the stolen conversations in the world. The writer as Burroughs sees him becomes an intelligence agency. A "maker of sense" from a mass of stolen messages. The famous "Burroughs paranoia" is only his conviction that things are not as they appear. Cut-up is a kind of farming or mining: turning over layers to pick up worms or gold. When the dead are no barrier, it is possible to converse with anyone anywhere about anything anytime.

Cut-up, collage, and pop art have much in common with the activity of the ragpicker, the bag lady, the city pack rat, as they rummage through the overflowing garbage of the late twentieth century hoping to come up with something useful. Artists and advertisers both have an interest in what is found. They compete for the rejected, for that which has been lost, seeped between cracks, or used. Use gives things the character that makes them desirable: it is the only force that cannot be imitated by machines. Used clothing, for instance, bears the unique signature of its wearer, a being incapable of exact repetitions. If advertisers capture some lost meaning first, they use all its energy to sell things. If the artists get to it first, they destroy it to release more energy. But after it is destroyed, the rejecta goes to a second, higher level of rejection and becomes twice as desirable.

The necessities of collage have transformed the end of the twentieth century into a frenetic garbage hunt. The *used* has more than chic value: it is the product made more original than the machine can make it. It contains at a remove a human *feeling* that cannot be had anymore first-hand, because it is absent in the new. The modernist command was Pound's "Make It New." The postmodern imperative is "Get It Used." The more used the better. At a remove from several violent transformations, the object begins to *live again*. The hippies' Free Boxes in California in the late 1960s were remarkable not for the used clothes they contained but for the clothes used–put back–taken out–used–put back again. On the third generation of use, clothes were imbued with psychic substance, made into fetishes.

The Dadaists and the surrealists fetishized the common object because it was both endearing and absurd, but it is only after use that it can serve as an antidote to the infinite assembly line of the new. The only humanity left behind by this assembly line will be in the gaps of production, in the seams of the rejecta. The current answer to the endlessness of production is the making of fetishes from what production discards, from its *past*. Production knows only one direction: forward into the future. Its mechanisms for recuperating the past are not very well developed yet, even though advertising moves quickly to recover the emotional content of the past, especially nostalgia, which it vastly prefers to meaning. The artist's advantage is speed: making personal use of the world abandoned by the machine more quickly than the machine can recover it to make it part of future production. The key word is *personal* (schizophrenic).

Western artists have entered the world of the particular awed by the abyss between feeling and the infinity of production. The Central European refugee still has the luxury of a concrete beef with an idealized memory. The personal defense of the Westerner is made harder by the absence of the mythic authority of memory, so he transcends time via drugs, geography via visa, boredom via art. A sloughing mechanism begins to operate as soon as meaning is raised from the garbage: the discourses of economics and art criticism fall to give way to warmth, to a different reality from that of the machine (one closer to mystic rapture), and to a whole range of forgotten sentiments. The productive shell of the ragpicker flows with the assembly line into the future, but the collagist-fetishist soars through schizo-sentimental sputtering into the Outside.

Communal living in the 1960s, the cut-up collage of utopianism, demanded an artistic point of view just as earlier experiments called for a religious one. But the religion of art had already collapsed with the Dadaists. The surrealists tried quickly to put the fear of art back into the people. It was too late: the bourgeoisie was first shocked, then it looked for ways to use shock to sell things. Looking at the world as art involves an instinctive grasp of collage, something the post-TV generation certainly possesses but lacks the will (or strength) to subvert (or understand) the dominant message.

There is another area in which surrealism triumphed in America, an area I will call the Chinese box. Raymond Roussel's novelistic fantasy, *Impressions of Africa*, is a Chinese box of infinite depth: the book has seemingly no end. The Chinese box is the crystalline structure of the body and of the universe as seen on LSD. Its emotional, intellectual, and physical immediacy makes the Chinese box one of the best vehicles for transport available. Ubiquitous, free, accurate, this universal transport system is always on time and always there when you need it. The traditional Chinese box is the "synchronous" I Ching ideogram, as Jung named it. There is no need to resort to literature: literalness does it. The Chinese box is also the place impossible to escape from: treadmills are all based on this principle. The Chinese box will take you to every Outside imaginable while revealing to you—at the precise moment of arrival—the profound structural interiority of the place you have entered. Your "seeing" is immediately rewarded (or punished) by the incorporation of what is seen. This glimpse and crystallization is what goes by the name of Beauty. It's an unbearably melancholy spectacle but the human adventure is predicated on it. Literature is both the search for and the record of these Outsides. (Sacred texts are here included.) Our century has greatly speeded up their discovery. The original glimpse of the Chinese box traveler becomes the path on which others will travel. The settlers come more quickly, too. The glimpsed Outsides do not take long now before becoming the maze boxes of the authorized world. A sinking feeling (the last feeling) assails one when contemplating the arrival of the police in what was once the nearly virginal vision of the unknown. The artistic adventure is one of circularized impotence when one realizes that vision is only the institution before the institution.

The Chinese box makes a sound that is variously magical: chant and incantation. From these seeds rises the commerce of music. The chanting of "primitive" ritual is also the sound of the Chinese box. The invocations of gods and ancestors, the sacred songs of tribal peoples, are the accompaniment of travel to the Outside. Dada and negritude—Caribbean French surrealism—have both used the hypnotic transport of the chanted syllable. Our use of "primitive" song is often merely precious and artistic, and the native is only a figure appropriated by "ethnopoetics." For all that, traveling inside the Chinese box is possible, if one can navigate between professors humming nonsense syllables like large constipated birds sitting on the eggshells of the ancient world and the zombied youth in the stoned auditoriums. The professors hatching the eggs of the anthropofied native are pathetic surrealist objects waiting to be collaged, anthologized, and museumified. The armies of the young are pinned like numberless specimens to charts. Cash and nostalgia are difficult to avoid.

The technically rich arsenal of surrealism was set up to "assert our complete *nonconformism* clearly enough so that there can be no question of translating it, at the trial of the real world, as evidence for the defense." The surrealist revolt was not going to allow itself to be misinterpreted as anything but a powerful *J'accuse!* "Existence," as Breton said, "is elsewhere." The adversary position of surrealism, in the form of a pure NO, is the surest antidote to the deadening of its own impulses. The Pursuit of the Marvelous, the Abandon to the Unknown, the Pleasure of the Strange, the Delirium of the Forbidden, the Deliciousness of Taboo, the Wisdom of Terror are fundaments of a poetic existence, which is to say a necessary existence. That promise has kept its appeal and continues to issue its siren song, despite the recuperating power of centers. It is in the nature of revolution that its promises are more inspiring, more generative, more fertile, and more ingenious than its adherents. If we should keep the surrealist spirit fresh, we must overthrow the surrealists as resolutely as if they were the enemy.

At a certain point—in, let's say, 1929—it must have seemed to André Breton and his Parisian circle that there were only two divergent orders of operation in the world: the Western bourgeois and the surrealist. It must have been a beatific moment, like looking upon the sight of a brand-new world from the mast of your caravel and seeing the unfolding of every possibility. The great, brutal, alien civilizations within the new land are as yet invisible, and so is the whole spectrum of disease, mortality, and sorrow waiting for you to set foot on land. Politically, surrealism is somewhere to the left of Trotskyism and slightly to the right of Royalism. It exists, that is, between the Trotskyism of Benjamin Peret and the royalism of Salvador Dali. And yet one can watch surrealists scurry to dogma: Eluard and Aragon give up poetry for communist propaganda. Tristan Tzara becomes a Stalinist. They did not abandon surrealism; rather, surrealism abandoned them. The surrealist spirit is exactly that, seizing humans the way big winds seize property. Our time has eliminated all compromised labels, whether Dada, surrealism, communism, or other isms. There is flexibility in being nameless and able to name oneself any time. To remain in a state of virtuality, open to possibility, the way one was before being put in the onomatopoeic cage of Proper, Christian, or Official name, is a de-adjectified right. On the other hand, being nameless (without language) leaves one prey to the image and to the labels of ever-changing fashion. Contradictions become inexpressible, possible only as tones of voice. The true oppositions between reality and simulacra, between the original and imitations, are described by the same names. The artists dig for the difference—but the Outside exists.

When the surrealists came to America in the 1940s to escape the war, they came to New York, which is only Europe with a great deal more energy, a Europe with an erection. The few of them who made it to California, or to the New Mexico deserts, probably saw that there was little reason for surrealism to continue in its didactic form after 1949. Barry Gifford sees it this way:

> "You must remember," says Desnos,
>   only one eye open,
> "this highway is a manifestation
>   of the route of Apollinaire."
> "Yes," says Breton, "beauty
>   is no longer a nuisance."
> "Or," adds Aragon, "a dream."

This has a rather naïve and, no doubt, shaky assumption in it, namely, that concrete instances suffice by standing in for what used to be adventures of the mind. And yet, what else is there? Western culture? After World Wars I and II? The ease of one's ancestors reposing in books was, thankfully, missing in this country. The past could not be taken for granted: it had been deliberately forgotten. America had no memory. People, including the surrealists, came here to forget. Everything had to be remade, everything was for the first time, everything was new. Mistakes would be repeated, horrors duplicated—but one's experience was the sole measure. A body, a place, a world: the work.

$$
\begin{array}{c}
P \\ A \\ R \\ T \\ \\ S \\ E \\ V \\ E \\ N
\end{array}
$$

How to
Become a
Better
Romanian

The apotheosis and destruction/ triumph of French surrealism and the unspeakable fate of futurism-become-fascism hold this lesson: the Balkans are an alternative to the self-destroying machines of modernism, to modernity itself—but without recourse to either conservative nostalgia or totalitarian terror.

Futurism was the encounter of German romanticism with the machine, the encounter of Goethe with the Model T. French surrealism was the encounter of French Romanticism with the Balkans (Dada), the encounter of Baudelaire's Poe with Tzara's sewing machine. It is no coincidence that futurism (as vorticism) was, through Ezra Pound, the dominant Anglo-American modernism. The adversaries within futurism and French surrealism are the Machine and the Balkans. Futurism, its automobiles and airplanes in motion, heads full speed toward the lone figure of an absurd bourgeois creature with a derby on his head who has, luckily, just left his body. Those two face each other across the poetic person of Arthur Rimbaud, who is now one, now the other. When he writes "The Drunken Boat," he is the levitating bourgeois. When he gives up—to sell guns in Africa—what is revealed is the thumping of the machine piston. And later, when Tristan Tzara gives up Dadaism to take up communism, what remains is a laughter spasm, a vapor of black humor.

I have been often labeled a surrealist by people who wouldn't know a surrealist if one came steaming out of their mouths at a French restaurant, and not only by them. What people usually mistake for surrealism is a different way of speaking. The metaphorical echoes of Romanian into English sound surreal. By that token, anyone sounding strange to a listener is a surrealist: we are all each other's surrealists. Given the increasing strangeness of human voices compared to media voices, we are all becoming surrealists. In a world inhabited by involuntary surrealists, silence becomes a real alternative. But I am not a surrealist: I am a Romanian, an exile. It is true that much of the European avant-garde between the wars was a creation of provincial Romanian Jews, chief among them Sammy Rosenstock, a.k.a. Tristan Tzara, but that is only a by-product of Balkanism. Balkanic exilism is distinguished by the fierce speed of its self-affirmation in the midst of fragmentation: each fragment is still within the explosion. The art of "meditation in an emergency" is our art. We speak a language propelled everywhere by paradoxes, little vehicles really, modes of historical transportation we have had to evolve to survive, as Romanians, at the crossroads of Great Power ambitions, and as Jews, of course, at the crossroads of anybody's ambitions. These paradoxical and vehicular means of transport bear the same resemblance to certain surrealist devices that bats bear to butterflies. Only the crudely uninitiated would confuse the two. Everyone is crudely uninitiated. The polished surface of generalized ignorance in our time allows for them only a handful of labels. Surrealism is one of those (safely historical), Dada is another (volatile). We live in a sorry state of indiscriminate assumption, made grosser by our crude good health. Acquired, may I add, upon the vomitous engorgement of the world, including its store of ever-thinning revelation. Carbon dioxide emissions and fluorocarbons are smothering the earth just as the remaining forests are being depleted by beings who write with light on computer screens.

Surrealism? I wish. Will the earth be fit for human habitation? Will humans be fit to inhabit themselves? An international treaty on stratospheric ozone is under way. No such alarms are being raised about the way we die inside. Will nomadism be possible in the age of climate control? Is nomadism forever doomed to the periphery, to an outside growing farther and farther away? Are humans the actual *something* at the edges of the universe that pushes out? Are we nevermore to know the warm old center? Is expulsion from the womb final? Does Poe's bird have the last word? Can we revolt effectively against the efficient interior from our scattered and exploding points on the edges of space? Can we give in to the constantly promoted blurring of distinctions between inside and outside? Including the collapsed textual ones? (Derrida is Dada with a couple of added Rs.) Was our generation the last to look out the window? Was it a mistake? Did the window blow open because of some machine's malfunction? Is there no third way after fundamentalist imprisonment within the book and soulless technology? These are urgent questions. Time is not on our side. (The Rolling Stones lied.) But the answer to at least some of these questions is yes. Yes, there is an alternative to both theocracy and technocracy. The solution is poetic. The main job we've had in the Balkans is to stay alive when it seemed impossible to do so. Nature abounds with extraordinary ruses, mostly mimetic. Taking on the color of machines is not easy now: they come in all colors. But they are still stupid, even linked in the projection of inevitability. The notion of history must, once more, be rethought.

For a long time we have thought of history as human history, even when it was being made by machines. With Karl Marx we began to think of it as a succession of machine forces organizing humanity in certain mechanical configurations. Marx narrated human history in the language of the machines. Our historical centrism was lost along with its language. A different retelling is in order: the anonymous history of the machine must be told in human (poetic) language. We must sabotage both the sentimental story that ends in God and the machine story that ends in the tool. In order to do that, we all of us have to become poets. (Not hard: we are already surrealists.) But we must become poets quickly, while it is still possible to speak. Before the vacuum of the mass sucks in the words forever.

The strategies of speech now may involve other mediums. We must rethink our relation to the image: Is it possible to speak through it? Indeed, does it speak? We know that words can point out even as they are being pointed in. But are images anything but self-referential?

Art, as it looks now, seems little more than the vanguard of real estate. Art galleries set the stage for gentrification of all the old neighborhoods in American cities. Artists become merchants. The popularity of art increases. There is art on the walls and in schools where people can see it. If there is any transcendental value in contemporary art, it is located in the upturned eyes of a seemingly baffled public. By looking beyond the obvious for what isn't there, the redemptive power is affirmed. This heartens the market, while it gives the critics an audience as well.

Other side effects include vast numbers of new subscribers to art magazines. Print proliferates all around. But how does art fare? If there is such a thing as art (rather than artists), it is probably suffering the shock of lazarization. Only a few years (pages) ago, art was dead. You could read its epitaphs everywhere. It has come back to life and it is having quite a shock trying out its grave-atrophied legs.

If there is no such thing as art, then the discussion returns to a dangerous place: the artist. The artist is a critical consciousness operating in time, a worker for whom neither money nor ideas is everything. At least, that's what one hopes. But what if there are no more artists? What if all there is is art? What if art isn't dead but the artist is? That would leave us only capital A Art, Art as a collective endeavor of ideological origin, produced by a number of appendages called "artists."

These workers are dead, in the all-but-productive sense of the word. They produce the raw material for the currency of ideas that Art circulates. For this, they get fed the modicum of electricity needed to survive in the damp of the grave. Art, in its collective totality, describes the shape of the future: it is the picture of it. Beyond the stage of present-day simulations of the real there lies that new world of extraordinarily varied simulation where the real has completely ceased to exist. In its stead, there appear the artistic minutiae of proliferating simulations. The new baroque is here: the surrealist nightmare incarnate. If the baroque is here, can God be far behind? If images can be made part of the poetic speech of historical sabotage, there is considerable hope. I have my doubts: look at the quick loss of subversiveness in the sexual imagery from modern art to modern advertising, and at the slow loss of every meaning from the icons of communism. Words are hard to iconify, though Power has tried: "Communism with a Human Face," "The War on Drugs," "The Moral Equivalent of the Founding Fathers."

To become a highly skilled saboteur of history is a job that involves a continuous meditation on the enemy, which is time, whether circular, digital, or atomic. Escaping from the interior of time into the outside of being is a necessity of both personal and collective survival. The job is also to stay sane while staying alive, something done best through division, a process sometimes known as schizophrenia. It is not easy being a saboteur, a fool for health, and a schizo-activist all at once. The surrealists encouraged neurosis, it is true, but they recoiled from schizophrenia, as their fear of Antonin Artaud clearly shows. As a schizo-activist, at least one of me disapproves of the surrealists. But what I have just described isn't a poetic, or not *just* a poetic. It is also the old Balkanic Levantine wisdom that protects the individual from history.

Here is the practical way the old-fashioned poet did it:

> I sell myths, not poems. With each poem goes a little myth. This myth is not in the poem. It's in my mind. And when the editors of magazines ask me for poems I make them pay for my work by passing along these little myths which I make up. These myths appear at the end of the magazine under the heading ABOUT CONTRIBUTORS or above my poems in italics. Very soon there are as many myths as there are poems and ultimately this is good because each poem does, this way, bring another poet into the world. With this secret method of defying birth controls I populate the world with poets.

And here is the practical demiurgy of the new everyperson poet:

Imaginary Beings

At birth, an Imaginary Being is very much like a newly born Infant. But unlike the Infant he grows not by being Fed but by being Spun. A solicitous mother will bring her Infant to the Age of Sex by constant Feeding. A creator will bring her creature to the Age of Sex by constant Spinning. When a powerful Vortex is created, the Imaginary Being releases another. Unfortunately, this kind of Vortex is achieved only in a culture where no one questions the morality of Imagination.

Everyone has, at one time or another, pricked a yogi with a needle and watched the sperm come out. But this is where most folks stop. In trying to populate the world with Imaginary Beings, most people fail, and many should not attempt it at all. Most of you are capable only of populating the world with a single being which is half-handed to you by your parents, with the other half culled from hypnagogic impressions. This is as it should be because not many can risk their minds at the hands of the two Fears: flying and public opinion. Public opinion has always been against Imaginary Beings of all sort but never as much as it is today. The first order of business today is the elimination of imagination for the total protection of the Single Identity Person. Anyone possessing more than one identity is immediately thrown in a hospital where the 'weaker' ones are severed. In most of these cases, of course, the stupidity of doctors eliminates the original identity while releasing the Imaginary Being, and thus Imaginary Beings survive *vole volente*.

But one day, in the heat of persecution, a pall

will descend over the persecutors, grinding the reductive technology to a halt. The fossil fuels will have run out and 'realistic self-appraisal' will have become suddenly bankrupt. At that time, the few of us who have patiently invented and stored Imaginary Beings, either inside of us or in secret attics and cellars, will have something of a tremendous advantage, an advantage I propose we seize in revolutionary fashion to put a whole new set of fantasies in the myth basket of the race.

W e are allies of the surrealists because we find useful the surrealist insistence on the "scientific," the insistence that its findings are objective. We can glimpse in this borrowing from the machine both the possibility of a personal defense and the endowing with character of imaginary creation. Why not, one may ask, simply educate the *real* children so that they won't play the current game of power? Because real children are educated through fairy tales: our culture tells the wrong stories. We must tell other stories. These "other stories" are our "other children," the educators of "real children." It isn't possible for "real children" to exist without "imaginary children." Schizo-activism cannot exist without relentless investigation: this is where its imagination is being employed. We do not want to abandon the Outside but to reclaim the interior's attention before it folds completely into its black hole. The hope of contact with the creative mystery is not a nostalgic hope of return. Strange mechanisms occupy the deserted centers now: we do not want to reinhabit them but we do not want them to dispose of us. We must not only change the direction of speech but make sure that ontological reminders are erected within our crossroads and tended by our inventory of fantasies to remind us of our original mandate (OM), which is to keep the universe alive. Which is to be in a state of grace induced by no matter what means, but especially through shock, although we must recognize that in our time shock has come to mean simply "intelligence."

The only shocking thing in our world is its fearless use. We must eroticize language, ourselves, the world: make the points of contact glow. This may have to be done unsentimentally now, when the war machines are the real sentiment machines (a tank is a hankie) and beautiful to boot. We must preserve the human nomad forms in all their *désuété* charm: gypsy scholars, misfits, politicos, truants, escapees, runaways, stewardesses, bus drivers, train porters, itinerants, night managers, self-born-agains, by-themselves, hired guns, Kelly girls, corporate fixers, nurses, malcontents—the drifting globe. Prophecy, which is the triumph of aphorism, should become a greater mode of speech. We should build an oracular and practical language on the blocked flows of political exiles while retaining the formal liberty of art. We should be capable of conceptualizing our experience to the point where it becomes new experience. The borders of the Outside are our immune system: its work is to defend the individual and give it shape at the points of contact. We cannot allow either the oceanic feeling of the great collectivity of the outside (fascism) or the alienating work in the interior (machinism) to do away with the human body. "The body is the plan," said poet Robert Creeley. Personal defense must be a defense against information overload as well. We should wage a campaign against too much information, like the campaign against cholesterol. Down with info-fat! The battleground is no doubt America, the paradoxical continent of Walt Whitman and Henry Ford, of the fascist-in-exile Pound and the stay-at-home globalist William Carlos Williams. Clearly, we must defend a kind of collectivity against a kind of individuality. And vice versa, clearly.

The
North American
Combine:
Moloch and Eros

"**A**merica is to be kept coarse and broad. What is to be done is to withdraw from precedents, and be directed to men and women. . . . The genius of all foreign literature is clipped and cut small, compared to our genius, and is essentially insulting to our usages, and to the organic compact of These States." So Whitman to Emerson in 1856.

In 1967 I met a hitchhiker on a country road in California whose sole possession was a tattered paperback of Whitman's poems which he had been carrying across the continent. He gave me his book before he thumbed his next ride. Whitman had traveled with this boy from Michigan to Oregon to Alaska and back. Here was the Whitman essence: two boys on the road to self-discovery passing poetry to each other. Implicit in that exchange was an enormous contempt for definition and possession, since the two boys knew not where they were going and they cared little for things other than those that fed their spirit. And the tattered book was more than symbolically appropriate: it was the right size. Whitman said: "I want no aristocrat editions . . . all my own tastes are towards books you can handle easily—put into your pocket. . . . That would tend to induce people to take me along and read me in the open air: I am nearly always successful with the reader in the open air." The air was undoubtedly open at that crossing in the second half (barely) of the nineteenth century. It began to close almost immediately.

Whitman's open secret is sex. Sex is also America's open secret since the very beginning. One can say that all colonizers are sexual deviants. Sex becomes the major preoccupation of people who leave home, for whatever reason. The need to preserve and redefine the family in unfamiliar surroundings demands constant thinking and rethinking of sex and sexual roles. To the Europeans, the wilderness and its inhabitants were an expression of naked sexuality. The wilderness had been functioning this way ever since distinctions were drawn between nature and civilization. The two met on the sexual border whose constant redefinition was essential to its maintenance. In the colonies this maintenance was exacerbated and the sexual questions became exaggerated.

The history of America can be told as a story of sexual pathology. The Puritans burned their witches to prevent indiscriminate coupling. The westward migration was an escape from the traditional family. The Civil War was rooted in fear of Negro sexuality. The Mexican-American wars were battles between two colonial philosophies: creolizing Latin colonialism and British clan purity. The world wars that followed were to prevent the Huns, German and

Japanese, from raping us. One can go on, primer-style, infinitely, without being wrong. The paradoxical aspect of this history is that it had the very opposite effect. Burning witches brought Hawthorne, Whitman, Emerson, and Thoreau into being. The westward movement gave rise to the loose sexual mores of the west, which gave birth to Hollywood. The Civil War broke down the social and racial barriers of the nineteenth century. The Mexican-American War created a creole border. The two world wars took Americans into the international community, where they came into contact with the philosophical libertinism of Europe.

America's industrial might and the sense of well-being it produced was translated immediately into sexual freedom. The emancipation of women speeded up the process. The technologies of the New World are intimately connected to its sexuality. They form a new couple in which all the struggles of partnership are reenacted. The human-to-human struggles are mirrored in the techné to human relationship, but there are new elements. Techné begins by liberating its human partner and ends up as Moloch enslaving him/her. "Him/her" is in significant order here. Techné/Moloch begins by enslaving men and liberating women. In the end it possesses both.

The riddle is: What is it about sex that isn't sex? And the answer, of course: sex theory. When the Austro-Hungarian Empire exploded it sent forth a million thinking seeds whose dirty work is far from finished. Each of these seeds, one of which is Mr. Freud, carries with it a burning desire to investigate the Big Bang that gave it birth. This investigation is the relentless sexual light that they shine on all things and societies among whom they are active. As outsiders, these seeds' job is to get inside to fertilize the native ovum resting placidly in the deepest interior. The only way to unsettle the ovum is to remind it that its job is to generate and reproduce, an activity possible only in the light of a philosophy that maintains the urgency of the task. I know because that is what I, too, a late seed of the great Empire, have been doing since I got here. And you who have stayed with me this long, it is too late to close the book. We will make a baby together.

The symbolic story of anything is sexual. Stories themselves are. People are stories. Countries are stories. Written history is, obviously, *his* story. Hers is Anonymous History, as told by Sigfried Gideon in *Mechanization Takes Command:* the automated kitchen, the assembly line, the equal opportunity job. Women and gender going, alas, out of style as differences are erased rather than preserved and enjoyed. Machines are androgynous, never mind their "male" and "female" plugs (terms borrowed from us, to make them seem "human"), and it is their androgynous needs that we serve at the cost of our differences. We offer our gender differences to the androgynous machines for the unrewarding rewards of "comfort." An illusion, at best, and the very opposite of Ease, which is to "comfort" what human is to machine.

And here is another riddle: What is it about sex that isn't sex? And the answer: literature. If America and its literature were gathered under the generative sign of this seedling's need to explain sexually, the picture (in words) would look something like this:

After Whitman and the transcendental New Englanders, what happens? Nothing or almost nothing until the 1920s, when a few American poets make contact with the European avant-garde. Even then, not a whole lot happens. Ezra Pound, in Europe, established a poetic dictatorship that managed to ignore surrealism altogether. He substituted for it something called imagism, an offshoot of vorticism and futurism, a poor cousin of those continentals.

Vorticism was proto-fascist, pro-energy, and pro-machine: it wedded Fordianism to the collectivist aspirations of an idealized Volk. Imagism was a proto-objectivism that quickly degenerated into sentimental tableaux. Fortunately for America, Americans have little patience for collectivist-nationalist fantasies. They are absorbed by the particular and value the individual. It was only with William Carlos Williams that things began looking up, but it was a long time before American poetry claimed for itself the kind of authority European poetry had always had. Pound attempted to deprovincialize American poetry by infusing it with bits of Chinese and other exotica, but his didacticism was a retreat from the scope of Whitman's vision. The coarseness and broadness of America found no room in American poetry until the 1950s, when Allen Ginsberg let them back in. To Europeans, American literature after Whitman is the American novel between 1920 and 1950. Even Whitman belongs in some sense to prose, not to poetry: his vast, capacious verse is full of landscapes, stories, and politics. Poe is the Europeans' only American poet, and he is Baudelaire's Poe. The American Poe is the Poe of stories. The American novel initiated Europe to the originality and vastness of America. The American language in prose was vigorous, capable of envisioning a continent that was still in the process of being made. The quality of attention that the American novel paid to the world was remarkable to Europeans, for whom prose had become decadent and vulgar. A Romanian poet friend once said to me: "If you ever write a novel, I'll never talk to you again!" The reality of our world was known to us only too well; we had consumed its bitterness detail by detail: the only thing left was escape, poetry. Prose to us was the unbearable world of the present, the living in history. We could not conceive of a world in whose unfolding we could take pleasure. Not so for Americans: their world was new, and there is a natural affinity in the language for prose, for exactness, for realism.

In North America words wrestle with things. We are no longer in the world of great events: the Fall in Time, the Mythic Meteor Shower, the Memorized Nation. Words as things cannot stray very far here from what they refer to. Language is chained to the world: contracts are written to that effect. The Sisyphean, purgatorial mode of this business arrangement is the writer's curse and blessing. A curse because it is difficult to go through every single thing in order to arrive at the other side where the being is released from things (and words); a blessing because the world can be charmed (made manifest, energized) by language. The horizontal dimension of the American of commerce and industry contrasts sharply with the (primitive) poetic vertical of a language like Romanian, spoken against things. Where American seeks to clarify, Romanian seeks to establish a climate, to make common cause against the world. Romanian is metaphorical, onomatopoeic, lyrical, exaggerated. American is brisk, precise, honest, factual. Romanians often talk for the sake of talking: a form of song. In America only jive and rap compare to it: marginal areas of the main linguistic zone. Romanian is antihistorical. American is all action.

Learning American was my introduction to the world. Where I had turned away from things before, I now had to face them and say, How do you do? Instead of soaring immediately above the point, I had to speak to the point. My introduction to American poetry was the New York School of poets. The New York School was in the Whitmanic tradition of American poetry, a tradition that stressed the newness of America and demanded total attention to one's circumstances. After Ginsberg's reopening of Whitman's gate, an American poetics was in place by 1966, the year I came to the United States. That was the year Frank O'Hara died, leaving to the coming decade the possibility of a genuine American surrealism. The things before me, in their brilliant and horrific richness, were said to constitute the world. The world did not have to be invented: it existed in full, baffling mysteriousness in the quotidian and the actual. One had only to stand in midtown Manhattan at rush hour to realize the truth of that assertion: the energy of things was more than enough. One swooned in its wake; one had to move to keep up. What made my encounter with the New York School fortunate was that, in addition to the exalted attention to place and time that the New York poets insisted on, O'Hara had introduced surrealist humor (subversion) to poetry.

The world of things had thus been visited by the militant imagination. Ted Berrigan, whose mentor had been O'Hara, said to me that "a poem, to be any good, has to work at least in four dimensions: sideways and up and down." I knew about up and down. Sideways worried me: there was so much material world in the New World, I staggered. How traverse it all and still rise? How be responsible to all that I see and still experience the sublime? Ignore nothing, and yet see its shining structure and the heavenly glue of its molecules? It had to be done: there was no place to go. "The poet," said Rimbaud, "by long and well-thought-out disordering of all the senses, must make himself a criminal in order to arrive at the Unknown." And so it was that light—shining through every single thing—made its way horizontally and vertically through the decade. We were the sleepless generation. And we had Poe's alcohol, Baudelaire's hashish, De Quincey's opium, Freud's cocaine, and the Nazis' amphetamine to complement our uniquely generational marvel: LSD.

I n North America the problem of finding a reason to write is infinitely more urgent than finding something to write about. The *why* of it is the
work. The *what* is pleasure. To put a new country on the
map, one must be ontologically assured of one's place in the
sun. (Or assured of its absence, its presence in memory.)
North American writers don't have that luxury. The problem is rooted in the social status of the creative writer, which
is to say no status. This is a productive (still) society and its
values are the measurable ones. The old European high
culture was a plaything of the rich, and when the Dada
revolution came, the rich became Dada. In America it is easy
to create a new social expectation by explaining that the
heads of statues must be cleaned: a need would arise,
instantly, for both head sweepers and pigeon killers. Social
expectations can be raised at any point, about anything: any
formal structure with an ego (cash) can create a vast need for
itself. Pet rocks and dirty jeans fulfill imperial ambitions.
The market is infinitely compatible. Then why did the
American imagination—which isn't lacking ambition—fail
to create a need in society for the poet? Why did American
poets, since the very beginning, have such a colossal inferi-
ority complex vis-à-vis such monuments of usefulness as
the Union plumber?

The American poet, until recently, would rather have
been anything else: geographer, chronicler, anthropologist,
politician, bureaucrat, or professor. The poetry Whitman
called for came and went in the 1960s, part of the adversary
culture, classifiable with drugs and pacifism and free sex.
During that decade, the outside was the domain of poetry.
The poet was the eminent outsider, and it seemed briefly
that America would at long last accept its poets as it has
accepted its other outsiders: western outlaws, frontiersmen,
and religious fanatics. But in the decade beginning in the
mid-1970s, something happened: "poet" became an accept-

able word and "poetry" became a civil-service job funded by the State and the academies. In the 1980s the American poet was legitimized, not at the dignified level implied by the phrase "a place in society," but at a lower, white-collar professional rank. The poet-professor appeared, an ominous courtly figure whose presence signals the death of poetry. The coarseness and broadness of America disappeared once more, leaving in their place gentility, fearfulness, and smallness. The encounter of surrealism with the New York School, which had produced a hospitable climate to an exile like myself, gave birth to dozens of dispirited translators.

What caused the passage of poetry from a powerful outside in the 1960s to an inside ghetto in the 1970s? Two things: the American suspicion of the imagination and the appearance of a new mandarin discourse that needs to annex poetry to legitimize itself. The American poet's traditional fear of the imagination met the open poststructuralist maw.

By 1977 I much preferred the newspaper to literature. The 1960s in New York had seemed to me like the fabled decade between the the two world wars in Bucharest, another golden age. Romanian intellectuals of that generation had been a prolific and diversified bunch: newspaper polemicists by day, café warriors in the afternoon, tavern visionaries by night. Bucharest between the wars was the place of a thousand cafés, each one with its own poet and each poet with his own newspaper.

The Romanian poet felt himself to be a *world*. The fertile encounter of Byzantium with the West produced a kind of cornucopic giddiness. That, and the fact that between the wars there had been relative liberty and lack of censorship. When the Communists came to power and I was born (events not necessarily related in *that* order), liberty disappeared but the urge stayed behind. Something similar befell

American poetry after the Vietnam War, silencing all but the organically incapable of silence.

In 1966 the Lower East Side of New York was a boiling cauldron of instant publication. The amount of literature that passed between my hands in one day was staggering: mimeo calls to mass rallies ("Let's carry a coffin to the Bolivian Embassy!"), mystical revelations fresh from LSD fountain-pen-cum-carbon, poems written and delivered on the spot, endless newsprint, feuilletons, manifestos, and even pure and simple but poetic advertisements for hippie merchandise in its pre-imperial phase. Over this jiggling sea of unself-conscious ink there stood the (by comparison) solidly anchored and majestic islands of the mimeo month-lies and the occasionals: "C," "The World," "Fuck You: A Magazine of the Arts," "Adventures in Poetry," and others. That was as complete a world of expressive assault as anyone could have wished. And yet, at the age of twenty, even all that seemed to me somehow *insufficient*. What seemed more like it would have been a publication that was like Ted Berrigan talking.

When Ted talked, he sent out magnificent shoots of organic connective material that wove as they illuminated. I was looking for a way for *poetry* to do that. The poetry I wrote at twenty was an amalgamation of fresh impressions of the New World poured into the sentence arrangement of contemporary Romanian poetry fashionable at the time that I left. My experiments in Romania with the poetic sentence had found a lever in Lucian Blaga, our great meta-chilling poet of almost cryptic, short lyrical stabs, who had, besides, lived in my hometown. I could have used Blaga's discoveries to leap forward into a kind of choked lyricism. But I had natural surrealist sympathies and I was determined not to let the Balkans down: after all, we had originated Dada and given voice to the absurd. Proto-surrealisms of various kinds floated about us since the symbolists. I was temperamentally and genetically suited for New York in the 1960s: the stuff in the air begged for the stuff in me. I had *more* in me: lots and lots of stuff to say or that wanted saying and there was no way that it could say itself in the Blagan sentence. So I was lucky to emigrate into the last flowering of the Beat Age and hear both the American imperative ("no ideas but in things"—W. C. Williams) and the brief song of freed poetry.

Ginsberg's "Howl" (1961) let the poet out of the cage of the artistic pout where the avant-garde had stuck him until then. The stance (sentence) that the Objectivist poets had worked out was so severe, so rigorous, and so insistent on the integrity of the line that only a monk (or somebody with another job) could renounce everything for its sake. American modernism, from Pound on, had traded in fierce asceticism. These days, in the oppressive boredom of the new Mandarin Age, we might well wish for the discipline of any high-minded art. But back in the early days of the 1970s— the decade of disco and computers!—I felt that the American moderns needed an infusion of surrealist humor. The New York School of Poetry had humor in abundance and a surrealist sensibility that matched mine. I came home in Frank O'Hara, Kenneth Koch, John Ashbery, Ted Berrigan, and all the others, and their painter and musician friends, too. I came to America exactly twenty years after Ginsberg's break with the short line of Williams in "Howl," a momentous, clean fissure: the lines of "Howl" unwind like coiled spring, and Whitman's America (grown horrifying and atomic in the meantime) burst out of them with the new sound of a new age. The age had other sounds, notably Bob Dylan's, and those of poets and musicians at various airborne junctions of the *esprit du temps.*

There were other sounds, mainly of commerce and ambition, mixed in with the dying of the decade: the whining of the coming age of professors. Overstatement, inflation, megalomania, bathos, and blather invaded the streets. They connected (stretching toward it) with the new age of consumerism that demands an "artistic" freshness from its relentless products, the ultimate of which is the art object per se, either one of a kind or something *like* it, which is the one-of-a-kind look of mass-produced fakes. Ginsberg's diction and the diction of Dylan, the Beatles, the Rolling Stones, and others all rushed to meet the inflationary future, sometimes as adversaries, sometimes as lovers. There was also an increase in true content, more often than not. Ginsberg's line, by approximating the newspaper (even though delivering the "underground" news), unwittingly allowed back a kind of academic/political rhetoric that became, in mild editorial form, the tone of much mainstream poeticking. This was perhaps why Williams (modernism) had insisted on such formal stringency. The rapprochement with the newspaper, democratic medium par excellence, was not accidental. The key to the poetics of the new age was in the *idea* of the newspaper, both as collage and as information. The newspaper is the demotic poetics of America. No poet can get around it. It is possible to look at America's greatest poets as publishers of their own newspapers. "The news that stays news" (Pound) gets out on a certain scale: it *publishes*, it *broadcasts*, it journalizes.

F rank O'Hara created a poetry capacious and energetic enough to accommodate everything in the poem: talk, literary posing, love notes, dreams, and occasional verse for his friends, all in a kind of eclectic daily diary, surrealist wall gazette–style. His work rejects old arguments between "formalists" and partisans of *vers libre* because it makes use of all available materials. All is grist for the mill. O'Hara does not shy away from drama, melodrama, gossip, or New York life as he lived it. His poet is an electric creature, as Apollinaire had once envisioned, with a telephone to his ear. The encounter in the late 1950s and early 1960s of New York poetry and painting was immensely beneficial to both. Language became more plastic and powerful, and art became more intelligent and subversive. A radical critique of the image was at the center of both arts.

Ted Berrigan got the music of spoken American into his line without relying on images. He trusted the spoken to come up perfectly, if perfectly synchronous with the intention to make a poem. The ear is mightier than the eye. The surrealists, who knew that something was wrong with the eye (Dali and Buñuel razor-Xed it), solved their unease by going after impossible images, but images nonetheless. Berrigan said, only half-jokingly: "I have no imagination." By "imagination," he meant precisely the image-making facility that dominates so much of contemporary life. Not having this "imagination" was for him a triumph: language doesn't paint pictures, it makes sounds. Like the newspaper, its job is to deliver the news. If images are evoked, that's a side effect. They're not intended. One of Ted's delights was the sports page, not only because he loved sports (he did) but because he liked the menagerie: lions eat saints, padres rip cardinals, tigers cream blue jays. Furthermore, if the poet is intent on the language, the perfect poetic sentences are bound to present themselves. Since they rarely come in bunches, they are to be stored in a basket in that funeral urn by the foot of the bed, until it's time "to compose." All the poet has to do then is to collage the perfect things said at one time or another, on the street or in history, and make a poem out of them.

Andy Warhol, Berrigan's friend, was the first painter to abandon the image. The ready-made preexists: it does not require a fresh assault on the eye. It demands an interpretation if forced by the context. Warhol and Berrigan forced the context. Warhol put the commercial in terms of art. Berrigan put the *moments* of speech in poetry. The weakness of the American poet is not that he has no imagination, but that he does not love poetry enough to *think on its behalf*. Berrigan tried to think his way through collage, just as Warhol did, just as the newspaper does. But he, unlike Warhol, suspected that collage wasn't enough. Which is why he talked like he did, connecting everything in ways that would have exploded the page if a way could have been found to accommodate such vibrancy.

The poetics-talk connection came via Charles Olson/ amphetamine. Charles Olson, via Pound, had been insisting on "breath" as the measure for the line: one breath, one line. He composed, as did many of the "Black Mountain" poets in the late 1950s, by venturing forth "in the field," the field being anything the poet was capable of using to make sense of. The New York poets, like the Beats and the Black Mountain poets, redefined the cultural space of America by making it more like America itself: varied, complex, multicultural, nonacademic.

Berrigan the talker was the perfect poet of the late 1960s. He was contemporary with his times and he was contemporary with himself: he was fast. The gap between the contemporaneity of the talker and the edge of the poetry was bigger at that time than the usual gap between life and poetry. Life had become suddenly huge and poetry rather small. The overflow of publications was partly an attempt to bring the poetics more in line with the dimensions of the age. All those pamphlets, fliers, and feuilletons were needed so that life wouldn't race too far ahead of expression. Ted was a "rhizome" (Deleuze), a potato that connected with whatever would connect with it. He even assumed the *shape* of a potato. His poetics, like Olson's and O'Hara's, made the most out of the surge of energetic slang in the midcentury, a politically and socially propelled slang filled with raw power. Hipster jive and hippie talk had power because they were illegitimate. When people *talked* in the late 1950s and 1960s, they were being subversive. Anyone still involved with the poetics of the image was in big trouble. Even the modernists' canon of weights and measures seemed insufficient. But there was only so much that the streets could put out, and Berrigan soon came up against the limits of that, and against the limits, as well, of the new Mandarin Age.

At a certain point in the mid-1970s, Berrigan's rhizomes (and those of other poets as well, including myself) put out the shoots but did not meet the organic shoots of future rhizomes: they met the crafted fittings of the literary biz. The coming age of discourse hit hard at the assumptions of hip speech, just as the age of advertising had all but disposed of imagism. The current degeneracy (legitimation) of the poet can be traced directly to the necessities I mentioned: the need to make Williams's line more capacious and Ginsberg's line more accurate. Berrigan's (written) solution was insufficient, and the mainstream found a perfectly innocuous line between the two, corresponding in size, taste, judiciousness, and plainness to the perfect middle-class "poetry graduate."

Berrigan's subtlety, and Olson's, and O'Hara's, was to see the extent to which a new poetics has to be made by every new poet. It was O'Hara's and Berrigan's fortune to live in a time and place (the 1960s in New York) that was aurally rich and technologically stunning enough to highlight the transition. This was also their misfortune: the new relations demanded new analyses. The technique (collage, drip-drip) could not stand in lieu of thought. A critical push was needed.

The language poets looked askance at lyric and song, leaving those poetries to others. In some sense, the only completely successful lyrical poetry in America is the poetry of songs, especially Black American blues. The reason for the hopeless floundering of academic poetries is precisely the insistent presence of Black genius for musical poetry. Hipster jive, as well as hippie talk, was based on Black speech. The metaphorical potency of Black American is like the metaphor-making powers of my native Romanian. All people under the gun invent ways of escaping history through language.

Poetry is an art of the Outside, where it best flourishes. In America now, poets have become marginally legitimate without having been illegitimate for very long. Our sojourn in the Outside hasn't been long enough. The new production rippling under the NEA/MFA/MLA umbrella is not benign. It is becoming imperative to restore both grandeur *and* honesty, always an impossible task. Current literary journals are, for the most part, tepid affairs: they are either organs of an institution or propaganda for a résumé-building subgroup, and are generally financed by the government. The new "small press" has merged with the academic quarterlies. Most writing today appears headed for the résumé, its final resting place. The institutionalizing of American literature is in full swing. Succession by edict is *almost* the only kind. Despite the historical adversity between academia and outsiders, the distinctions are blurring. A general diffusion is taking place. The extreme (self-professed) avant-garde of the "language" school is merging with the academia and the National Endowment for the Arts like the trash compactor walls in *Star Wars*. The *esprit du temps* is a stubborn *objet*. In the age of information, the free-floating traffic of poetic language cannot be tolerated. It must be controlled. What better way to do so than by using the surrealist "method" itself, a device as effective as translation and drugs?

Certain books reinvent literature because they could care less about it. They aim at overthrowing the human race and at remaking the world. "All writing is pigshit," said

Antonin Artaud, the schizophrenic. "I salute him," said Henry Miller of Blaise Cendrars, "because he is an absolute traitor to the race." "Poetry demands unemployment!" says one surrealist manifesto. "This is the time of the assassins!" Rimbaud claims unequivocally at the birth of the modern world. Echoing Henri Michaux, Ted Berrigan aims straight: "Some people prefer the interior monologue! I like to beat people up!" And William Blake, a jagged rock on the well-trimmed lawn of English literature: "Sooner murder an infant in its cradle than nurse unacted desires." At times the craving for vision, for the outside, is so strong, the delicious cry of "To Hell with Culture!" echoes through the world. (Herbert Read, who uttered those words, was unfortunately arguing only boring Marxist agitprop.) This is one of those times, a time choked in the weeds of academic and civilian formalism. To put it mildly, most of what we see in print in North America is unbearably trivial and singularly devoid of courage. "Eroticize the proletariat!" says Gherasim Luca. We would if we could find it. And to Allen Ginsberg's "America, go fuck yourself with your atom bomb!" the spirit of the times seems to cry once again, Fuck, yes! Darrell Gray says: "I will not pay taxes until Fuck is used widely on television!"

But metaphorically and *literally*, America has stopped fucking. Language is partisan to whatever makes it shine. It is not an independent deity, nor is it a blissful automaton. It is a follower, a violently partial mistress of the way the wind blows. In America, the wind began to change in the mid-1970s. Until that time, language could be made to glow with the love of self and there seemed to be an intimate connection between the glories of the body and the seductiveness of speech. The prevailing tone was one of the poetic physicality of Rimbaud's vowel tonguing, and of Whitman's macrovision. All this was under the sign of the left. Today left and right do not represent political realities any longer but emotional states. In the 1960s it was obvious, to the point of appearing to be "the natural order," that language was with the people. Not so. The people it turned out were infinitely more unsettled than originally supposed. They were sick of the body, and many of them longed for the public body, for age, wisdom, and strong authority. The disgust with the political process and the wish for simple clarity also reflected a distrust of the Outside, a rejection of the metaphysical and a new desire for the comforting routine of the interior. The complexity of how things really are, the frightening figures, the economic dryness, the environmental nightmare, the nuclear horror, are no longer part of mainstream discourse.

In literature, the old directions long ago lost all meaning. To speak of left and right in letters is to evidence the naïveté of the old left. The urge for ideological definition, for a taking of stands "on issues," reflects only a desire to transcend the current critical approaches to art. Or the lack of them. The desire for critics is itself a desire for a return to order, a sign of the times. Successful writers these days cultivate the language most apt to ignite the flame, that is, the clear and unambiguous language of the right. Wrestling with the old experimental problems now is the desperate act of a rejected lover who humiliates him/herself to get the lover back. There is little that is more embarassing. *Postmodernism* is the polite term for getting on with it. The abrupt withdrawal has created tragicomedy: the poetic authorities have been left on their couches with extinguished pipes. It was not—it never is—language in trouble. Language is the opiate: in the end, the sick light is on the junkie. Meanwhile, the new discourses roll in, particularly Neo-Marxism which appears to have decided to annex all modernism and postmodernism. Its dialectical tanks are at the moment rolling over everything in their way, a veritable Brezhnev Doctrine of discourse. Practitioners of the "language" school,

Marxist Neo-Dadaists, are likewise involved in the effort of destabilizing the extralinguistic claims of poetry. The problem of the "language" school, however, is the problem of all avant-gardes today. What was once fresh is downright torture, and the reason why the avant-gardists revolted in the first place. Discursive neo-romanticism (nostalgized gauchism) shows signs of growing rather than abating, thanks to academia, where every failed strain of the avant-garde, usually embodied by the lone practitioner, the Teacher, is being played out.

The specific psychological and social angers of the left decades of our century (the teens, the thirties, the sixties) had magnetized the linguistic lines of force so that it appeared that language, writers, and the people were going the same way. Language must be seduced again by a forceful poetic/critical discourse. The critical discourse must become part of the poetic discourse. The poetic must make clear the thinking that connects it to the world. That demands a certain clarity and polemical stance that have been lacking from the timid, grant-fed, university-sponsored American literature of late. The absence of discussion, scrutiny, and talk has made possible an extraordinary inflation of poets and poems. The world's most secret art has now become a vast waiting room, in an airport perhaps, with thousands of people milling around being "nice" to one another. A rite became a cult, then a religion, then a certificate mill. Only no airplanes seem to be landing or taking off, and the mysteries of the rite have become rather banal exercises having to do with prosody, line length, and so on. All that has been gained by modernism in its exploration of the world through language, since the last decades of the nineteenth century, is now being made innocuous by the new interior.

The
NewAge,
Before
I Forget

The central issue of the so-called New Age, the child of my age, is No Age. The desire to live forever and be forever young is also the oldest human longing. It belongs to everyone, which makes me suspect that living forever is possible, not just as an icon or a book or a series of tics in a number of children, but as the actual body that you find yourself at present in love with. In a story by Mircea Eliade, someone speculates that cancer may in fact be the elixir of immortality because its job is to make all new cells. Its problem is not knowing when to stop after making, let's say, a perfect new liver. Cancer suffers from ontological amnesia. It has forgotten when to stop. If only we could teach it, we would live forever. Teaching cancer the forms involves drinking a certain water from a certain spring. . . . Back to Ponce de León, and Florida, where my mother lives and organic farms flourish, all of them motivated by the same old story.

Chaos research, now conducted at Los Alamos, involves the descendants of the original disintegrators of matter in such activities as watching faucets drip and flags flapping in the breeze. They are hoping to identify the order underlying so-called Chaos. The nonlinear reactor spewing fractals holds out the hope of a New Order. This mathematically ideal solution could then become an obedience school for such chaotic forces as cancer. You could send cancer or a hydrogen explosion to Fractals High and the result is Chaos working for a living.

The guilt-ridden A-bomb makers are in fact trying to prove that there is no such thing as Chaos. If the Chaos they unleashed when they rent asunder matter is only a different order, accessible mathematically, it is theoretically possible to understand it, and in some way *take it all back*. They would like to cure their guilt with understanding, that great palliative placebo of the Age of Reason.

In reality, there never was such a thing as Chaos. As anyone who has taken LSD knows, the symmetry of matter is maddening. Absolutely everything is structurally beautiful and dizzyingly perfect as well as infinitely repetitious, whether it's a diamond or a pile of dog shit. Matter does not exist: what we perceive is the rhythm of energy flows. The slow flows are pictures, the surging flows are, well, beyond that. The fast flows are like the deadlier rides at the amusement park: the body can barely stand them, the strain threatens to blow apart the edges. The point of Chaos research, or any research for that matter, is to slow down the energy flows enough to translate them into mathematics, which in turn can be translated into machines. The machines regulate energy, so it would seem that they are potentially as infinite as the energies they regulate. Immortality is thus just around the corner. As is the great inevitable beauty of the atomic blast. In truth, energy is increased by speed. The faster it moves the more energy is created. Energy slowed down is energy destroyed. Our translations are energy-negative.

The human means of increasing energy is desire. Thus our entire effort has to be predicated on the dynamics of desire. My compatriot Dracula had a problem with desire. He discovered immortality but found out that the real problem was inventing ways to stay interested in life. The maintenance of desire was an endless and terrifying job, solved neither by aristocratic elitism (only the young and rich deserve to live forever) or by art (movies). Dracula was doomed to stay in the world long past the point where it amused him. In other words, he had been granted his desire to live past the point where he had any desire. The point where desire ceases is the point where entropy sets in, and energy begins to flow back into a black hole. Nothing is good enough for the immortal: the energy of the world feeds endlessly and desperately into the black hole of his boredom. The black hole is not generative: nothing *more* is created, everything is lost. In order for more to exist, for the universe to be generative, it is absolutely necessary to stop at the point where energy ceases to be moved by desire. In other words, it is absolutely necessary to give up the energy-destroying vision of immortality. If cancer knew where to stop we would live forever, like vampires, but we would become cancer itself, a malevolent force that would do to the universe what cancer now does to the body. We would be energy that has lost drive, will moved by the inertia of an energy-destroying ideal. Between immortality and immorality stands only the cross of a T: lest ye die, *nothing* is going to live.

The recent space-shuttle explosion was caused by badly baked O-rings supplied by a polygamist manufacturer in Utah. Our most advanced technology was unraveled by a baked zero sent into space by jealous polygamists wrapped in an earthbound battle for power. The zero shape of the O-ring is significant. It is the symbolic shape of the feminine principle contested by the warring polygamists.

The guilt of the Los Alamos scientists is significant in the same way. It is the element that binds the original destruction to the search for order in chaos. It is the desire to make good what was bad, to take back the original act.

The amnesia of matter that New Agers are seeking to cure is also born of the desire to improve the originally corrupt nature of human beings. The desires of polygamists, Los Alamites, and New Agers are highly suspect because they would go to any lengths to submit the actual to the ideal. Only the actual has the ability to gauge the state of energy flows as they occur. The ideal disregards the points of change, stasis, loss of desire: it is eternally faithful to itself. The jealousy that sabotaged the space program, the guilt caused by the blowing up of a million humans in a mathematically perfect blast, the utopian urge, are all by-products of the ideal.

Giving up the ideal for the real is our only job. Recognizing the point where the creative urge is stilled is our basic moral dilemma. Surrendering at that point the symbolic aggregates of matter and self is morally the right thing to do. Morality is giving the crystallized images of captured energy flows back to the universe. Wanting to live forever is immoral, just as it is immoral to destroy energy still possessed by the desire to be, just as it is immoral to circumscribe the desire of another. That is why immortality (Dracula) is evil, Los Alamites are guilt-ridden, and Utah polygamists are bad. Morality is the secret knowledge of every organism of its exact relation to desire.

The moral unease of scientists, utopians, and cultists provides the fuel for research and discovery. Without that guilt, no nonlinear reactor. Without that vision of immortality, no organic farms. Without that jealousy, no perfect baked zeros.

The New Age, in all its multifarious manifestations of hopefulness, from afterlife fantasia to confabulated community, is a body of research for the underlying order in Chaos. It is also the splintered and commodified (merchant-capitalized) result of the great single-wave philosophical realization of the 1960s that Chaos does not exist, and so neither should alienation, death, or suffering. The single realization of the makers of the A-Bomb was its unparalleled destructiveness, a realization that splintered into various kinds of current research. Likewise, the New Age is the practical laboratory for an Original LSD-induced Vision. The question before us is how to maintain those revelations in an actual rather than an ideal state. Or, if you prefer, how to liberate research and discovery from the exigencies of Original Sin and Utopia.

What interests me is the maintenance of the moral dimension of these researches before they get translated into machines. I don't want to be immortal, sure of order, or able to remember everything. I want to get things going faster even if that means giving them up. Knowing when to give them up is the special wisdom that makes room for the renewal of desire. Like the rest of my generation, I'm not exactly sure how to give up the dead old world without reinventing it. But when I feel the clean blade of the Original Anger, I remember.

The Disappearance of the Outside

My friend Greg, a professional philosopher, just bought his first computer. Millions of words have been written about the changed relations between writer and writing because of the computer. In spite of them, every new user has to talk about it. It is a *fin-de-siècle* rite of passage, an initiation into contemporaneity. "I used to look out the window a lot when I wrote," Greg said. "Now I find myself looking at the words I have just finished writing."

"Very soon," I said, "you will not need the computer to see words on a screen. There will be words on a screen *everywhere* you look. They will be the words you just thought." I should have said, "the words you just thought you thought."

With the computer, the philosopher's window disappears. He will be staring henceforth at his own propositions.

Interiority has taken command. Insofar as Greg is a *professional* philosopher, the computer only formalizes a *fait accompli*. It is only amateurs who feel keenly the loss of the sky.

What Greg had been seeing out his window had been rapidly diminishing in any case. Even the great rain forests of Brazil are under attack. It is possible that if Greg had been an amateur he would have seen these forests, and perhaps all that is left of the wilderness standing there before his window in mute supplication. His window would have looked onto the places where the roads don't go. Even then, he would have seen them only through the glass, Mies glass no doubt, the fetish of modern art that separates the eyes from all the other senses. It is not only the wilderness that dies outside Greg's window, it is also the sensual life of humans, our own inner outside.

The computer screen completes the last turn to the interior. "The word," William Burroughs said, "is a virus." The word, to be more specific, is the virus of interiority. The computerized word is interiority squared. The word on TV = the word x the image of it. The way out of the mirror is cut off.

In the past ten years the Outside has greatly diminished in all its dimensions: geography, imagination, liberty. Transcendence has closed shop, or perhaps the last room in a shop that has been closing since the Renaissance. But even simple escapes are no longer simple. One can no longer simply walk away anywhere but only into proscribed zones, wastelands between freeways, culs-de-sac under floodlights. Even science fiction is distressed by our premature arrival unto its territory: it has become nostalgia fiction, a gleam off the tail fins of Edsels and Sputniks. The unknown, once accessible in various ways, has been sealed off at the borders. The police have arrived everywhere: in the East they are uniformed police. In the West they are the invisible police of image manipulation. The militarization of the planet is complete—"There are no more civilians," says Paul Virilio—and that of outer space is well under way. We have been drafted against our will like peasants in the Middle Ages, dragged off to war without even noticing it. Power goes unquestioned because our eyes are full of images that obscure it. Only rarely, and then without passion, does it occur to us that the brave new world of consumer goods is only the anesthetic before the great juggernaut of power. How can such useful and pretty things hurt us? The cult of the commodity has rendered everyone powerless while removing the critique of power to an abstract realm hard to connect with the (otherwise busy) senses. All the things that mimic human desires ("sexy guns") are in fact circuit breakers: they increase the need proportionally to the distancing of satisfaction. You can't *always* get what you want because you can *never* get what you want because you don't know *what* you want when you can have *everything that looks like it*. Desire itself eventually becomes false desire until its entire energy becomes the property (and fuel) of power. The simulacrum has everything except reality, the corpse of which it drags about the world until it can find a suitable way to dispose of it.

The world outside the Western borders has been closed *ahead* of the expansion of markets: the psychic enclosure now issues us a completely new set of eyes. Or maybe the markets have always been primarily psychic: the meta–blue jeans arrive ahead of the real ones. Drunk on imaginary Coca-Cola, the Third World wills itself into the production-consumption cycle at a point even more menial than that eventually reserved for it! The hastily erected walls of religious fundamentalism in Iran and elsewhere are belated attempts at nationalist quarantine. Mohammed, sword drawn and Stinger missile flashing, is dueling a fleeing pair of meta-Levis and the shadow of a can of Classic Coke. The fundamentalist enclosures create truly fantastic interiors where even the reality of a worldwide machine is denied, the better to befuddle the faithful.

In the crumbling bureaucracies of Europe, and in the Third World, the paper *dokument* still does the job, an old-fashioned paper symbol of a bureaucracy that dreamed itself merely infinite. Ah, Mayakovski, how you waved your red passport! Bureaucracy, in those early days after the Russian Revolution, looked briefly like a devastated amusement park full of tubular intestines and hallways with smashed windows and peasants camping out on the muddy carpets. It looked like a hopelessly outdated monster, the toppled dinosaur of Tsarism breathing its overly complicated last. But soon, almost immediately, the intestinal machinery began to breathe anew, expelling peasants and poets, painting the windows in lead. "The chains of tormented mankind," said Kafka, "are made out of red tape." And blood-red passports. And rusty-red barbed wire.

The new interior of the computerized *fin de siècle* is not the interior of the earlier decades. It is an interior that has learned to mimic some of the characteristics of the outside. It has learned, above all, to project a sense of inevitability. Few people are to be found anywhere who do not think that technology "causes problems" but "you can't stop progress." Fewer still who believe that bureaucracy is not eternal. The three-dimensional posters pasted over the windows of skyscraper offices open onto alpine vistas, Swiss snow, and edelweiss. Until now, human interiors had always been defined in relation to their fragility in the great cosmic outside. The womb, the cave, the house, even the armor, had been small markers of presence in a vast and wildly alive cosmos. All that is changed. Even without visual prosthesis, the new imperial interior has brought revolt to a standstill by projecting the innocent simplicity of its own control machinery. It is, of course, quite beautiful. It is endlessly connective, completely modular, always in the process of putting out a new branch, joining with another tunnel. It is also expandable in any given direction. The mechanisms by which we are made to do the things we do stand exposed before us. How could we harm these things of which we are a part? Things that we can *see*, including the part that we are? Even if the part we are is the part that gets endlessly relegated to a more and more marginal position? How can we protest the downgrading of the human when the human component is so clearly less adaptable, less predictable, less cooperative than the rest of the machine? How can we question the pristine evidence of the superiority of use? Are we not consumers of efficient use? Are we not users of abundance? Do we not benefit from well-regulated production? Do we not owe ourselves to the logic of use whence we possibly came and where certainly we now find ourselves? How can we steal when stealing will increase prices all of us will then be forced to pay? How can we attack a particularly vile war machine when this war machine defends *us* against another vile war machine? How separate the war machine from the industrial machine in general? Aren't shoes and bombs products of the same machine? Aren't humans counterproductive, nostalgic, and, anyway, inefficient?

The notion of community has been stripped of its direction. No longer does community—*any* community— stand outside the State, in direct challenge to it. All communities have been reoriented through a neat trick of generalization to *become* the State, an electronic Superstate that is a combination of traditional nationalism and electronic globalism. When community was a means of resistance, it was constituted to point from the inside *out:* it proceeded from a center of internal concerns to make progressively wider contacts with the outside world. The community redesigned by the State points inward: it is a producer of silence. Television has redesigned community life by pushing its electronic imperative into the center while marginalizing true community concerns. People find the hyperreality of TV more "real" than their own (unpublicized) life. They know TV families—the Nelsons, the Cleavers, the Huxtables—better than their own. The language of the media has become the *only* language, which is the same as having *no* language. The silenced, displaced centers of community life orbit about the desolate periphery like pieces of cosmic junk around a space station. The techniques by which the Western State has insinuated itself at the heart of community are visual. Red fascist bureaucracies in the East ensured their less productive interiors by closing tightly their borders. The uncirculated, stale interiors of the East compared unfavorably to the circulating, energetic, expanding interiors of mass-market societies. Those ex-Communist interiors are now in their final stages of bureaucratic decay: their structures are complex ruins whose inhabitants dream only of escape. The escape they imagine is inevitably into the West, into the Eden of TV. The East spills infrequently into the West, its inert material made active by boredom. The recirculation of interiors energizes both systems and keeps them growing.

As the interior becomes all there is, there is less and less to oppose to it. There is nothing to compare it to. The memory of the outside is also a form of interiority: the outside resides *in* memory. It can be argued that the interior is the space where everything disappears, including the bombardments of the media, that it is an active vacuum (or a series of vacuums, one inside another). Jean Baudrillard, in *In the Shadow of the Silent Majorities,* sees the mass as a black hole, capable of absorbing anything, reflecting everything, giving up nothing. The only thing that exists in the interior is a hyperconformism, a flattening out of all differences, a mechanical and collective mass that is either manipulated or manipulates the social, political, economical, and philosophical attempts on it. This kind of interior can only be the result of a new institutional nature, a rapidly growing projection of a new bureaucratic automatism that severs the organs of dissent, including, most importantly, the mouth. Hence the silent majority. This new nature has little to do with ideology, it is rather a function of the technological structures that now link everyone in a new electronic nervous system. The new passivity is the result of hormonal-electrical engineering. We are being fed salt-peter, on the one hand, and ginseng on the other. We are being castrated of expression but kept excited for consumption. That explains both the mind-boggling conformism of the mass (they all wear Reeboks) and the extraordinary empty physical vitality that possesses it (they all jog). Institutional nature substitutes itself for every aspect of older nature (or Nature), imposing its mechanical models on those of life, most often painfully penetrating the resistant *tissue* with levers and push buttons. The old organic connections were dependent on quantum leaps for communication, they were inseparable from what they became, they were in fact composed entirely (along their entire range) of awake (informed) substance. Life was unquantifiable in a way that is in question today when the machinery of the new nature has become so . . . natural.

The Outside is a substance increased and diminished. The Outside exists, most importantly and before anything, as *an appetite*. We are losing our appetites for everything: food, adventure, freedom. They are replaced by controlled cravings induced by visual and aural stimulation. At the same time we can see the diminishing of what lies outside ourselves, outside the feeble light of our cravings and their consumption needs. Fifty percent of the world's population will live in cities by year 2000. The other 50 percent will not have more room, however. They will be inhabiting pro-scribed areas on the edges of toxic pits. The environment will be rigorously gridded to serve the needs of the electronic brain. Every human being living now can see the shrinking of the world and feel the effects of relentless metering. We don't even need facts and figures to see. How do we see? In the same way that we *see* that no one is home before we even turn the key in the door, or sense the presence of an animal somewhere behind us without even turning. The animal is a machine and it no longer hides in the dark but it is always with us.

Rationalists may try to convince us that the Outside does not exist, but to deny the experience of it would be like denying childhood. The Outside is not simply what is uncovered by our needs in search for satisfaction, the way people sometimes think of "growing up" as an enlargement of the area of experience. Neither the Outside nor childhood are annexed zones of consciousness. They are not, either one of them, an unconscious. The Outside exists both in a physical, geographical dimension, as parts of our planet yanked out of their specific ecology and made to turn about the petty tyranny of our desires, and in a metaphysical dimension, as an area accessible by religious feeling. In its physical sense it is the place where the human creature is equal to other living things, where it operates ecologically in order to balance (create) the world, where it speaks with animals with or without shamans, where indeed it can forget itself. In its metaphysical sense it is that place of dreaming, accessible by imagination and poetry, where we have stubbornly insisted on going since we began as a species. This is the place of the original creative gesture, the apex of fertility where there is no difference between mind and matter. Every gesture made here is felt along the entire web of being, and every gesture has consequences. There are no mechanical blocks along the strands, the web is not broken by obstacles, borders, and holding cells. There are no impediments to travel (which is simultaneous anyway),

and escape is infinite and always generative. That the two embodiments of the Outside are disappearing together is the greatest tragedy that has befallen us so far, a tragedy much greater than an adverse history.

Separated from our own nature by a wall of Mies glass, deprived of the ability to become animals, or at least to speak with them, and of the mythical imagination (which takes refuge in smaller and smaller genre-ghettos like poetry, which themselves are being quickly colonized), we become no more than the slaves of machines, machines ourselves, slaves of slaves. The cybernetic view—that man is the splendid machine—finds no essential quarrel between biology and mechanics. The entire energy of the new nature would appear to support this view, but only up to a point. When man the machine comes into conflict with the machine-machine, the decision goes to efficiency. The communality of the species is enhanced by its functioning *more*, not less, like a machine. Marshall McLuhan, in *The Agebite of Outwit*, credits Gutenberg with the invention of the individual, but is not distressed by his demise in the new electronic globalism: "Literacy stresses *lineality*, a one-thing-at-a-time awareness and mode of procedure. From it derive the assembly line and the order of battle, the managerial hierarchy and the departmentalization of scholarly decorum. Gutenberg gave us analysis and explosion. By fragmenting the field of perception and breaking information into static bits, we have accomplished wonders."

The electronic media, however, operate differently. Simultaneous, auditory, global, tribal, connecting us all to the only job left: moving information. Work disappears. It will be done by the machines. But which machines? The *lesser* machines. We, the superior machines, will work at becoming more of a *single* organism. And more of a *marginal* organism. The individual dies for the species. The original program. Finis. But which species? Theirs or ours

McLuhan's vision makes no room for the unpredictable, th\
asystemic, the imaginary. It is a closed and closing circuit. It
cannot foresee its overthrow, and it knows nothing of the
operation of mystery in the world. It is not demiurgic, it is
cooperative. It conforms to its own ineluctability. The State
and rationalism (religion before that) have always attempted
and never succeeded in passing themselves off as irrevo-
cable, necessary, and ineluctable. It is the task of technology
as the newest member of this directorate to finish the job.

Those who dismiss the antitechnological revolt as mere
romantic nostalgia are not realists. They are agents of the
machines. The job of the human organism is to survive. It
will fend off any perceived threats to its integrity. The dread
and horror we have been feeling since the advent of the
Industrial Revolution are real. We have been seduced by
machines, it is true, but the last two hundred years have not
brought about an improvement of the species as a whole,
nor have they created a better, stronger, freer individual.
Mass conformism brought to its present-day apogee in the
silent (surveyed) mass will eventually cause humans to
abandon the planet. The planet (the Outside) is no longer
within easy reach: we sense it, like a memory, as it is being
murdered.

The Outside is sometimes increased in unexpected
ways. An excess of interiority can produce a wilderness. The
great European city is an interiority gone over to wilderness, an overgrown inside. When the city loses sight of the
central plan it becomes an organic entity, it reverts to nature.
Its doors are trees. A curious (and hopeful) reversal took
place at the extreme of commodification during the last *fin-
de-siècle:* the sensuality of the world of commodities became
generalized, diffuse, and uncontrolled. It condensed to
become an atmosphere within which the exchanges of the
past met in an unexpected way the pulses of the present.

The eroticized air began to listen to the dictates of its own ecology.

Eugene Sue's *Mysteries of Paris* discovered that one did not need to travel in order to find strange and mysterious things but could do so right at home in one's own city. But: (1) not every city is Paris, and (2) our *fin de siècle* is infinitely better guarded against such reversal. The only mystery of most twentieth-century cities is how one can endure living in them. Particularly in those made-for-the-automobile urban wastelands of shopping mall America where human beings are mere accessories of engines, textiles, and electronics. Statistics show that youth violence is endemic to many of these places, a natural response to the institutionalized dehumanization of the surroundings. Under the circumstances, alcohol and drugs are humanizing agents, agents of a dreadful kind of *sobriety*. Man has been deposed roughly from the center of things since the Renaissance. In his latest displacement he has lost the central city and the center of the city proper. The new cities-for-the-automobile have no centers: they are endless, circular periphery. Man's attempts at re-entering the shrinking, living Outside by regaining the center while escaping the marginal and constantly marginalizing interiors have been mostly sporadic, violent failures. The violence is inevitable, but as the policed interiors become seamless, the violence is increasingly against oneself. The hope held out by the nineteenth-century city's reversion to nature has had more recent manifestations in society and in the body. The same phenomenon occurred within a social class in the 1960s when the well-regulated middle class produced an aberrant generation of children who became voluntary "outsiders." Cancer, our contemporary psycho-environmental disease par excellence, is also a wilderness grown within to spite the ways in which we have abandoned the earth. The interior of body and society depends on stability, on reasonable rules. When these are overcome, the wilderness returns, like the jungle through the asphalt in Miami.

Two decades ago "the doors of perception" were blown wide open and flying became commonplace. There was seemingly unlimited space. Drunk on so much Outside, we took it for granted that our institutional life would soon be flooded by the infinite. We looked forward to *transparency*, to policy based on the awareness of light. Perhaps what we were experiencing was not the true Outside (it could hardly be, in view of all the already operational horrors) but only a glimpse of it through a briefly opened philosopher's window. What the glimpse revealed was the outside at possibly the same moment that it was disappearing. What lent substance to the glimpse was the ongoing war in Southeast Asia, a war marked by ecological and human "defoliation," a real mirror of new conditions. In the East, likewise, the Brezhnev Doctrine provided a fine syntactical view of the language of tanks: guns poking through the holes in ideas.

From the brief meeting of the transcendent with the historical there formed a certain critical authority, a certain weight. It was the palpable weight of this new resistance that almost amounted to a jail break. The personal, familial, and societal structures all felt its impact. The institutions began to close in, to defend the marked (marketed) territories. The approaches to the Outside were rapidly repressed, bought out, colonized, internalized, closed. The doors of perception were locked back up. The Oedipal doors were closed by worried parents with the hasty sacrifice of our generation. In tactical retreat, they wrote us off in order to save the younger siblings. A variety of techniques, from greater permissiviness to an increase of technical fantasies, were employed. Art was pressed into service. Its task: to create a world of strange new toys to keep everyone amused while the mending of fences and the repairing of walls took place. The next-to-the-last slice of the American economic pie rotated suddenly into view on the lunch counter. Everyone scrambled for it, trying to finish school, to fit into a suit, to get a job. The social doors in front of the Oedipal doors were shut by the police with new paranoid fantasies about morality and race. The geographical doors were shut by closing any but the approved tourist tracks. The twin policemen of science and religion were posted at the doors of Mystery. Gates to all experimental endeavor came clanging down all over the place.

The militarization of inner space was a two-decade project. The same agent was, in some cases, responsible for both liberation and re-entry. LSD 25, first introduced to civilians by the CIA, provided a brand-new psychic field for the testing of new internalizing techniques. The inside and the Outside, in the Taoist sense, are often interchangeable. They can, in fact, change places so fast, the being in transit is caught napping. Two decades ago, many young people, having gone to sleep inside, awakened under the stars. Today, the rare person going to sleep outside is likely to awaken in prison. Even skid row parks, those few tolerated areas where the destitute can sleep, are being increasingly closed. In the Soviet Union and Eastern Europe there was no question of sleeping outside, whether in the city or in what remains of the wilderness. The police arrested even those publicly overcome by drowsiness. The reconstructed universal prison of the 1990s is superior to the one we escaped from in the 1960s. The controllers know what to look for. But improved or not, the control valves that prevent the universe from flowing through us are still the same valves we had once breached. The brain, which is the valve room, was once bathed in the light of the outside. No amount of repair can straighten out the poetic damage to the bio-Oedipal-social cage. The State solution is the destruction of the

Outside itself, and of the only vehicles capable of reaching it: imagination and memory. Its job is the erasure of possibility, the absolute occupation of the unknown by what is known, the obliteration of mystery. The interiority of body, family, and State is waging jihad against the eternally generative universe.

The invasion of the Outside in the 1960s transcended politics. Until now, the approaches of the two major political systems were different, because the transports to be attacked demand different tactics. Memory had to be fought with a false history made so ubiquitous that what scattered individuals remembered only seemed fleeting and insubstantial when faced by the collective memory of the indoctrinated younger generation. Imagination, on the other hand, must be attacked at the root: it must not be given *time* to take flight, no takeoff room. The reduction of round, biological human time to speeding-up mechanical time is almost complete. Digital time is a pulse: by mistaking it for the beating of our own hearts, we mistake the demands of mechanical time for our own. Where does dreaming fit?

The attack on unauthorized memory is still waged with words, but imagination must be destroyed by the manipulation of images. This is where the quickly disappearing difference between the crumbling Soviet Empire and the West used to reside. Propaganda and censorship, those word-based methods of eradicating dissent, have failed spectacularly. Yesterday's dissidents are today's heroes in the East, but are they equipped to understand the devious oppressive power of image-based media? Until the recent revolutions in the East, the distinctions were clear: the Censor ruled that world, TV ruled ours. The Censor and the TV were the neat Couple in whose suffocating embrace the human slowly gave up the ghost. It now appears that the old Censor has dissolved into the illusionary liberty of our image-making machine. What happens from here on out is no longer a question of ideological oppositions, but a struggle for global reality. There are two global realities, resembling in a nonrepresentational way the old programmatic realities of East and West: the imaginary electronic globe, and the poetic-specific-eco-community.

The poet's job is to short-circuit the imaginary globe.

N O T E S

Page No.	Source

15   **This pamphlet:** In addition to the 1485 Leipzig pamphlet, there were numerous others, including reprints of German troubadour Michel Beheim's famous verse work *The Great Monster* (a new edition was published in Berlin in 1968 under the title *Die Gedichte des Michel Beheim*), and *Historie von Dracule Wajda,* a recently discovered pamphlet printed in Leipzig in 1493.

19   **"Proletarian Love":** I believe that the newspaper was *Flacara (The Flame),* but I am not certain. My paraphrase is almost certainly accurate since the yellowed clipping containing this masterpiece traveled in my wallet for years, and served as a prime example whenever the subject of our bankrupt literature arose in the café.

30   **twice ventured outside:** Eugenia Ginzburg, *Within the Whirlwind* (New York: Harcourt Brace Jovanovich, 1981).

31   **Our problems are completely incomprehensible:** Andrei Synyavsky, *Kontinent* (New York: Anchor Press/Doubleday, 1976).

33   **Invisible faces:** Ibid.

45   **These aborigines** and **in the course of almost one-fifth:** Vladimir Nabokov, *Speak Memory: An Autobiography Revisited* (New York: Putnam's, 1966).

45   **America was an uninterrupted:** Andrei Codrescu, *The Life and Times of an Involuntary Genius* (New York: George Braziller, 1975).

50   **Diagonally opposite:** Hans Richter, *Dada: Art and Anti-Art* (New York: McGraw-Hill, 1966).

50   **If it is agreed:** Terry Eagleton, *Exiles and Emigrés: Studies in Modern Literature* (New York: Schocken Books, 1970).

53   **The tiller is in constant conflict:** Felicitas D. Goodman, *Ecstasy, Ritual, and Alternate Reality* (Bloomington and Indianapolis: Indiana University Press, 1988).

55   **In the clear night of noon:** St. John Perse, *Selected Poems* (New York: New Directions, 1982).

61   **Never has the division:** Czeslaw Milosz, *Visions from San Francisco Bay*, trans. Richard Lourie (New York: Farrar, Straus & Giroux, 1982).

62   **In modern times:** Ibid.

64   **The world has become** and **The West has remained faithful** and **Wouldn't it be more in keeping:** Witold Gombrowicz, *Diary, Volume One: 1953–1956*, ed. Jan Kott with introduction by Wojciech Karpinski, trans. Lillian Vallee (Chicago: Northwestern University Press, 1988).

65   **the pistol with which:** Ibid.

66   **So long as Hitler:** Isaac Bashevis Singer, *Shosha*, trans. by author and Joseph Singer (New York: Farrar, Straus & Giroux, 1978).

67   **He loves them:** Roman Vishniak, *A Vanished World* (New York: Farrar, Straus & Giroux, 1983).

68   **What is the biggest:** Ibid.

69   Milan Kundera, *The Book of Laughter and Forgetting*, trans. Michael Henry Heim (New York: Knopf, 1980).

70   **My enemy:** Milan Kundera, *The Unbearable Lightness of Being*, trans. Michael Henry Heim (New York: Harper & Row, 1984).

71   **Franz had the sudden feeling:** Ibid.

73   **As the mass media:** Milan Kundera, *The Art of the Novel*, trans. Linda Asher (New York: Grove Press, 1988).

77   **I do not believe** and **Of eclecticism** and **a need to experience:** Václav Havel, *Letters to Olga: June 1979–September 1982*, trans. and with introduction by Paul Wilson (New York: Knopf, 1988).

79   **From the sketch to the work:** Milan Kundera, *The Art of the Novel*, trans. Linda Asher (New York: Grove Press, 1988).

198   Jean Baudrillard, *In the Shadow of the Silent Majorities* (New York: Foreign Agents Series, 1983).

201   Marshall McLuhan, *The Agebite of Outwit* (Albuquerque: Tuyoni, 1987).

203   Eugene Sue, *Mysteries of Paris* (New York: Howard Fertig, 1987).

80   **When nature disappears** and **What are the possibilities:** Ibid.

87   **the only English writer:** jacket of G. Cabrera Infante, *Infante's Inferno* (New York: Harper & Row, 1984).

91   **The world of amnesia:** Nicomedes Suárez-Aráuz, *Amnesis: The Art of the Lost Object* (New York: Lascaux, 1988), p. 93.

94   **interesting parallel:** Marcel Corniş-Pop, letter to the author, February 1, 1987.

94   **Have you noticed:** Christopher Carduff, letter to the author, March 15, 1989.

131   André Breton, *Manifesto of Surrealism* (Ann Arbor: University of Michigan Press, 1972).

135   **imagination which knows no bounds:** Ibid.

139   Comments on Niagara Falls quoted in Peter Conrad, *Imagining America* (New York: Oxford University Press, 1980).

140   Jackson Lears, *No Place of Grace: Antimodernism and the Transformation of American Culture, 1880–1920* (New York: Pantheon Books, 1981).

144   **What the Greeks did:** Gilles Deleuze, *Foucault* (Minneapolis: University of Minnesota Press, 1988).

146   **It is a bad thing:** William Burroughs, *The Job* (New York: Penguin, 1969, 1970, 1974).

153   **assert our complete *nonconformism*** and **Existence is elsewhere:** André Breton, *Manifesto of Surrealism* (Ann Arbor: University of Michigan Press, 1972).

155   Poem: Barry Gifford, quoted in Andrei Codrescu, ed., *The Stiffest of the Corpse: An Exquisite Corpse Reader* (San Francisco: City Lights Books, 1988).

162   **I sell myths:** Andrei Codrescu, *Secret Training* (San Francisco: kingdom kum press, 1973).

163   "Imaginary Beings" comes from Andrei Codrescu, *The Poets' Encyclopedia* (New York: Unmuzzled Ox, 1980).

167   Walt Whitman, *Appendix to the Leaves of Grass*, 1856 (New York: Viking Library of America, 1982).

170   Sigfried Gideon, *Mechanization Takes Command* (New York: W. W. Norton & Co., 1948).

173   Arthur Rimbaud, *Complete Works* (New York: Harper & Row, 1975).